782.111
B433m

MUSIC THEORY FOR MUSICAL THEATRE

John Bell and Steven R. Chicurel

D0792499

The Scarecrow Press, Inc.
Lanham, Maryland • Toronto • Plymouth, UK
2008

SCARECROW PRESS, INC.

Published in the United States of America
by Scarecrow Press, Inc.
A wholly owned subsidary of
The Rowman & Littlefield Publishing Group, Inc.
4501 Forbes Boulevard, Suite 200, Lanham, Maryland 20706
www.scarecrowpress.com

Estover Road
Plymouth PL6 7PY
United Kingdom

Copyright © 2008 by John Bell and Steven R. Chicurel

All rights reserved. No part of this publication may be reproduced,
stored in a retrieval system, or transmitted in any form or by any
means, electronic, mechanical, photocopying, recording, or otherwise,
without the prior permission of the publisher.

British Library Cataloguing in Publication Information Available

Library of Congress Cataloging-in-Publication Data
Bell, John, 1964-
  Music theory for musical theatre / John Bell, Steven R. Chicurel.
    p. cm.
  Includes index.
  ISBN-13: 978-0-8108-5901-2 (pbk. : alk. paper)
  ISBN-10: 0-8108-5901-7 (pbk. : alk. paper)
  eISBN-13: 978-0-8108-6364-4
  eISBN-10: 0-8108-6364-2
  1. Music theory—Elementary works. I. Chicurel, Steven R. (Steven Robert) II. Title.

MT7.B42 2008
782.1'11—dc22
                                                            2007052568

∞[TM] The paper used in this publication meets the minimum requirements of American
National Standard for Information Sciences—Permanence of Paper for Printed Library
Materials, ANSI/NISO Z39.48-1992.
Manufactured in the United States of America.

Contents

Acknowledgments   v

List of Figures and Compositions   vii

Introduction   xi

Part 1: Rudiments of Music   1

Part 2: Essays in Music Analysis   45

Part 3: Workbook   87

Glossary   101

Appendix: Permissions   107

Index   113

About the Authors   117

Acknowledgments

The authors wish to thank Andra Bell, Craig Carnelia, Justin Fischer, Karen Hiscoe, and Nancy Sullivan for their professional and personal encouragement; Patricia Borne for her editorial assistance; the University of Central Florida MFA musical theatre students in the Fall 2005 Script and Score Analysis class—Paul Gebb, Josephine Leffner, Chris Staffel, Michael Swickard, Debbie Tedrick, and Courtney Winstead—for being the "beta testers" of the book; and the University of Central Florida Faculty Center for Teaching and Learning for assistance with scanning and editing, care and feeding. In particular, thanks to Justin Delabar for his expertise and patience in helping us with things electronic.

Figures and Compositions

Part 1

Figure 1.1: Keyboard with pitch names   1
Figure 1.2: Semitones   2
Figure 1.3: Whole tones   2
Figure 1.4: Staff with chromatic scale   3
Figure 1.5: "Chop Suey," mm. 52–56, chromatic scale   3
Figure 1.6: Staff with diatonic scale   3
Figure 1.7: "You are Love," mm. 1–6, diatonic scale   4
Figure 1.8a: C-major scale   4
Figure 1.8b: B-flat major scale   5
Figure 1.9: "The Little Things You Do Together," mm. 29–31,
    ascending E-major scale   5
Figure 1.10: e-natural minor scale   6
Figure 1.11: e-harmonic minor scale   6
Figure 1.12a: e-melodic minor scale (ascending)   7
Figure 1.12b: e-melodic minor scale (descending)   7
Figure 1.13a: Major scale with scale degree names   8
Figure 1.13b: Natural minor scale with scale degree names   8
Figure 1.14: C-major intervallic scale   9
Figure 1.15: c-minor (natural) intervallic scale   9
Figure 1.16: Augmented fourth or diminished fifth   10
Figure 1.17: Enharmonic equivalents   10
Figure 1.18: Augmented fourth in a major scale   10
Figure 1.19: Order of sharps   11
Figure 1.20: Order of flats   11
Figure 1.21: Major key signatures   11

Figure 1.22: Circle of fifths   12
Figure 1.23: C-major scale and its relative minor   13
Figure 1.24: "King Herod's Song," mm. 1–4 and 9–16, relative key
   relationship   14
Figure 1.25a: C-major scale   15
Figure 1.25b: c-natural minor scale   15
Figure 1.25c: c-natural minor scale with key signature   15
Figure 1.25d: E-flat major scale with key signature   15
Figure 1.26: "Far from the Home I Love," mm. 5–16, mutation   16
Figure 1.27: "I Enjoy Being a Girl," mm. 53–63, mutation   17
Figure 1.28a, Figure 1.28b, Figure 1.28c, Figure 1.28d: Four triads
   built on C   18
Figure 1.29: C-major triadic scale   18
Figure 1.30: a-minor (natural) triadic scale   19
Figure 1.31: a-harmonic minor   19
Figure 1.32: "Chop Suey," mm. 1–4, parallel triads   19
Figure 1.33: Root and first inversion triads   20
Figure 1.34: Root position, first and second inversion triads   20
Figure 1.35: "Love, Look Away," mm. 5–9, parallel triads   20
Figure 1.36a, Figure 1.36b, Figure 1.36c, Figure 1.36d: Cadences   21
Figure 1.37: Seventh chords   22
Figure 1.38: "Side by Side by Side," mm. 29–32, 37–40, 63–64,
   examples of seventh and ninth chords   22–23
Figure 1.39: "Being Alive," mm. 20–21, 131–136   23–24
Figure 1.40: Tonic chord progressions   24
Figure 1.41: Dominant chord progressions   25
Figure 1.42: Subdominant chord progressions   25
Figure 1.43: Supertonic chord progressions   25
Figure 1.44: Submediant chord progressions   25
Figure 1.45: Multichord harmonic progressions   26
Figure 1.46: "I Don't Know How to Love Him," mm. 1–8,
   traditional chord progression   26–27
Figure 1.47: Simple chord-tone melody with accompaniment   27
Figure 1.48: "Can't Help Lovin' Dat Man," mm. 1–4, traditional
   harmony with chord-tone melody   27–28
Figure 1.49: Simple melody with nonharmonic tones and
   accompaniment   28
Figure 1.50a: Diatonic passing tone   28
Figure 1.50b: Chromatic passing tone   29
Figure 1.51a: "Christmas Lullaby," mm. 28–31, diatonic passing
   tone   29

Figure 1.51b: "Matchmaker, Matchmaker," mm. 35–42, diatonic
  passing tones   29
Figure 1.52: Anticipation   29
Figure 1.53: "Christmas Lullaby," mm. 78–85, anticipations   30
Figure 1.54: Retardation   30
Figure 1.55: Échappée   30
Figure 1.56: "You Are Love," mm. 57–59, échappée   31
Figure 1.57: Cambiata   31
Figure 1.58: "Sorry-Grateful," mm. 17–18, cambiata   31
Figure 1.59: Neighbor tones   32
Figure 1.60a: "I Enjoy Being a Girl," mm. 28–31, lower-neighbor
  tone   32
Figure 1.60b: "I'm Not Afraid," mm. 13–14, upper-neighbor tone   32
Figure 1.61: Appoggiaturas   32
Figure 1.62: "Can't Help Lovin' Dat Man," mm. 19–22, appoggiatura   33
Figure 1.63: Prepared appoggiatura   33
Figure 1.64: "Matchmaker, Matchmaker," mm. 3–9, prepared
  appoggiatura   33
Figure 1.65: Suspension   33
Figure 1.66: "Love, Look Away," mm. 5–8, suspension   34
Figure 1.67: Example of the V/V chord in C-major   34
Figure 1.68: Example of V7 chord in the key of C-major   35
Figure 1.69: "A New World," mm. 58–72, common-chord
  modulation   36
Figure 1.70: "Losing My Mind," mm. 59–61, enharmonic modulation   37
Figure 1.71: "Being Alive," mm. 73–77, abrupt modulation   37–38
Figure 1.72: "Ol' Man River," mm. 15–34, temporary modulation   38–39
Figure 1.73: Note and rest symbols   40
Figure 1.74: Staff with time signatures, bar lines, and rhythmic
  patterns   40
Figure 1.75: Whole rest in various metrical settings   41
Figure 1.76: Symbol for common time or $\frac{4}{4}$ symbol   41
Figure 1.77: Symbol for cut time   41

Part 2

"Ol' Man River," pp. 1–3   49–51
"Housewife," pp. 1–8   56–63
"Love, Look Away," pp. 1–2   67–68
"Stars and Moon," pp. 1–15   71–85

Part 3

Major Scales	88
Minor Scales	89–90
Intervals	91
Enharmonics	92
Key Signature	93
Triads	94–95
Cadences	96
Harmony	97
Functional and Nonfunctional Harmony	98
Rhythm	99

Introduction

At its most basic level, song literature represents a marriage—a lamination, if you will—of text and music. The combination of these two modes of expression creates a language that is unique and powerful.

Tools for understanding and then interpreting *any* language are diverse. Those for song literature come from the worlds of theatre and music. A composer writes for the theatre the way a playwright writes for the theatre, except the composer uses *musical* language rather than *literal* language. The goal is the same: to capture the essence of character and situation. Just as the playwright uses letters, the composer uses tones. The tones form chords (words), musical phrases (sentences), and musical sections (paragraphs). In the same way that a playwright builds dramatic interest through the use of rising action and *dénouement*, a composer uses the tools of dissonance and consonance to transport the listener on a musical journey.

Early methods of musical theatre acting training espoused the notion that singing actors should approach a song as if it were a monologue. Singers were encouraged to speak the text without music to investigate the lyrics' naturalistic qualities. Then the student was directed to add the music gradually, first as underscoring, and finally return to sung delivery. This technique, while valuable, perpetuates the dangerous assumption that the lyric of a song is the most important component of the song's dramatic expression, and places little or no emphasis on the composer's art.

This book addresses the role and value of music as a contributor to the dramatic *gestalt*, particularly in the musical theatre canon. Currently there is a dearth of literature that focuses on the tools the composer uses to complete the union of spoken word and music.

This book, designed to introduce the musical theatre practitioner to a new paradigm for musical theatre study, has three parts. Part 1 features elements of music theory that are basic for practical application to musical theatre songs. Part 2 contains examples from the musical theatre repertoire that demonstrate the lamination of music and text analysis. A supplementary section, Part 3, provides the educator and the student with practical drills in a workbook format.

It is important to note this book is intended *not just* for actors, singers, and dancers. In fact, based upon the authors' personal experiences using this model for song analysis, this book will be of great value to stage managers, designers, directors, choreographers, and musical directors. The authors believe the result can be a shared and specific working vocabulary that enhances the efficiency of the process (design and production meetings, rehearsal, etc.) and enriches the product (performance).

Most professional musical theatre training programs require that students study music theory. The content of such training, however, varies widely in both depth and rigor. Now that the number of musical theatre training programs has increased, so too has an awareness of the specific educational and skill needs of their students.

The time has come to ask a series of questions. How do musical theatre artists differ from traditional musical and theatre artists? Do the specific, day-to-day tasks in which the musical theatre artists engage require the full complement of music theory training? If not, what should be included? Is there a more logical way to sequence the information to reveal its direct application to the art form?

Some musical theatre students begin their university program of study with less musical preparation than drama or dance training. As such, they find themselves overwhelmed and demoralized as they try to keep pace with their more musically sophisticated peers. This book approaches some of these challenges from the point of view that, while musical theatre artists *may* need the full complement of traditional music theory instruction, a course of study that would apply the information more directly to the art form will better serve the actor, singer, and dancer as well as directors, choreographers, stage managers, and designers.

What do musical theatre artists need, musically? Lawrence Thelan's book *The Show Makers* reveals, through a series of interviews with some of the contemporary musical theatre's most prolific directors, that, for many, the ability to read music is not considered a key skill for success in the profession. Additionally, there are other musical theatre practitioners who would also assert the same opinion. After all, that's what the musical director is for, right?

In the authors' experiences, a basic command of musical language and its primary components *is* an essential "survival skill." The ability to read and analyze melody, harmony, and rhythm allows musical theatre artists to explore the composer's contribution to character and plot development.

It also allows directors and musical directors to discuss, as partners, musical needs regarding introductions, interludes, and transitional music. It assists actors in preparing excerpts for auditions. It enables choreographers to look at a score and recognize nuances or punctuations that they may want to capture visually. One of the potential and perhaps unexpected values of this text lies in its application to the training of stage managers, who must converse with other musical theatre artists. Stage managers will also benefit from the ability to understand musical language in order to facilitate calling musically specific cues. In short, the musical theatre artist is working in a theatrical form that is, after all, musical. Why would he or she *not* want to speak the language?

Music contains three basic components. *Melody* gives music its voice and shape, *harmony* gives music its aesthetic color or mood, and *rhythm* gives music its movement. These components combine to create the universality that allows music to speak to all people regardless of time or place. Further, when music is combined with words, the dramatic potential intensifies.

The authors approach this text with the assumption that the reader possesses a basic understanding of reading a musical staff, a knowledge base equivalent to an elementary-level course in music theory. Therefore, this book does not provide orientation to note names, clef, and other rudiments of printed music. In a classroom setting, this text can be useful in the study of musical theatre performance and musical theatre script and score analysis. This book will enhance the understanding of any teacher, student, or enthusiast who has an interest in musical theatre literature.

While it would be helpful to be able to play the musical examples on piano, it is not essential. The authors encourage the reader to listen to recordings of the songs from which the examples are taken.

Additionally, the authors believe that the study of music theory need not be intimidating. Armed with a few basic principles of melody, harmony, and rhythm, the musical theatre artist will be successful in creating, "page-to-stage," the world that not only the playwright but also the composer and lyricist have imagined.

It is the authors' hope that this book will prove effective both in independent study and in classroom settings.

1

Rudiments of Music

Melody

Melody refers to the succession of individual pitches used to express musical contour and shape. These pitches have letter names, A to G, and appear on the keyboard below (figure 1.1).

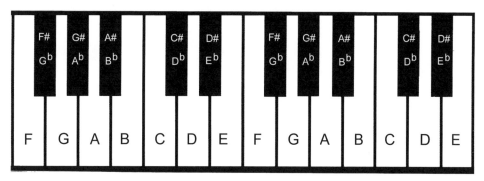

Figure 1.1. Keyboard with pitch names

The distance between any two adjacent keys is a semitone (ST), commonly referred to as a half step. For example, E to F and F to F♯ is a semitone (figure 1.2). Two adjacent semitones create a whole tone (WT), also known as a whole step. For example, G to A is a whole tone (figure 1.3).

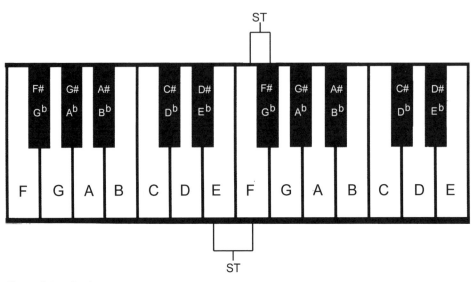

Figure 1.2.   Semitones

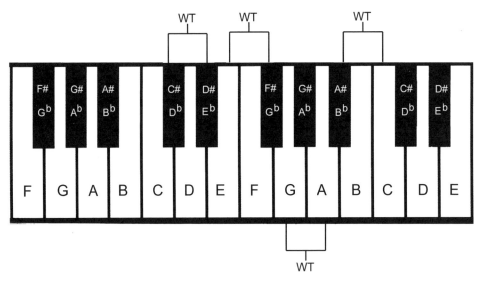

Figure 1.3.   Whole tones

Alterations to named pitches are called *accidentals*. A *sharp* (♯) raises a pitch by a semitone. Conversely, a *flat* (♭) lowers a pitch by a semitone. A *double sharp* (𝄪) raises a pitch by two semitones, while a *double flat* (♭♭) lowers a pitch by two semitones. A *natural* (♮) cancels a previous alteration. An accidental affects the note that follows as well as all notes of the same pitch within a measure.

A stepwise sequence of semitones or whole tones creates a pattern; whether in ascending or descending order, these patterns create *scales*. A scale that is built entirely of semitones is a *chromatic scale* (figure 1.4).

Figure 1.4.   *Staff with chromatic scale*

Measure 55 of "Chop Suey," from *Flower Drum Song* features a chromatic scale in the top note of the accompaniment (figure 1.5).

Figure 1.5.   *"Chop Suey," mm. 52–56, chromatic scale*

A seven-note scale built on a combination of semitones and whole tones is a *diatonic* scale (figure 1.6).

Figure 1.6.   *Staff with diatonic scale*

An example of a melody made up of diatonic scale tones appears in measures 1–6 of "You Are Love" from *Show Boat*. (Notice that the melody is doubled and reinforced in the accompaniment; see figure 1.7).

Figure 1.7. "You are Love," mm. 1–6, diatonic scale

Mode refers to the resulting color or tonality elicited from scales or melodic sequences. The two most common modes in Western music are the *major* and *minor* modes. They consist of eight notes. For purposes of this book, these two modes will be emphasized.

Typically, the major mode is perceived to be "positive," "bright," or "effusive," while the minor mode is perceived to be "negative," "dark," or

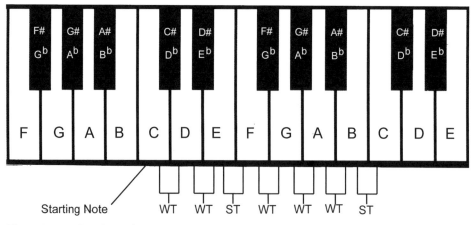

Figure 1.8a. C-major scale

"reflective." Reference to the major mode is notated by capital letters. Lowercase letters are used to reference minor modes. Therefore, an uppercase A represents A-major, and the key of a-minor is represented by a.

An ascending major scale has the following formula (this pattern is reversed for the descending scale): Starting Note/WT/WT/ST/WT/WT/WT/ST (see figures 1.8a and 1.8b).

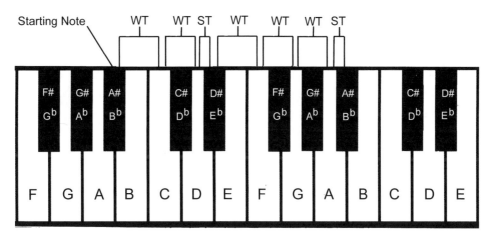

Figure 1.8b.   B-flat major scale

Stephen Sondheim outlines an ascending E-major scale in measures 30 and 31 of "The Little Things You Do Together," from *Company*. The melody begins on the second scale degree, the F$^\sharp$, and ascends to the high E (see figure 1.9).

Figure 1.9.   "The Little Things You Do Together," mm. 29–31, ascending E-major scale

There are three common forms of minor modes: *natural*, *harmonic*, and *melodic*. The natural minor scale has the following formula: Starting Note/WT/ST/WT/WT/ST/WT/WT (see figure 1.10).

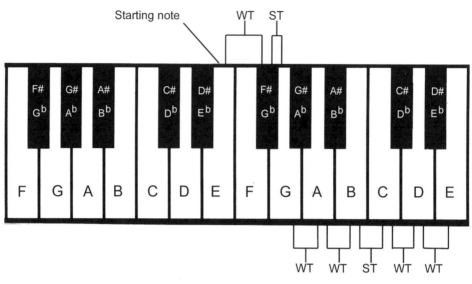

Figure 1.10. *e-natural minor scale*

The harmonic minor mode raises the seventh scale degree of the natural minor scale. It utilizes the following formula: Starting Note/WT/ST/WT/WT/ST/WT+ST/ST. Notice that the distance of the second-to-last interval in this formula is three semitones (a step and a half). Most Western melodies that are written in a minor mode are in the harmonic form (figure 1.11).

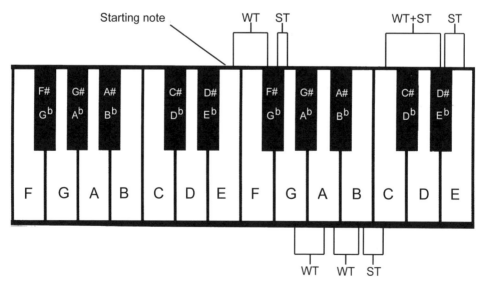

Figure 1.11. *e-harmonic minor scale*

The melodic minor mode raises the sixth and seventh scale degrees *ascending* by one semitone and then follows the natural minor formula *descending*. The ascending melodic minor scale follows the formula: Starting Note/WT/ST/WT/WT/WT/WT/ST (see figures 1.12a and 1.12b). Therefore, the descending melodic minor scale is the same as the descending natural minor scale.

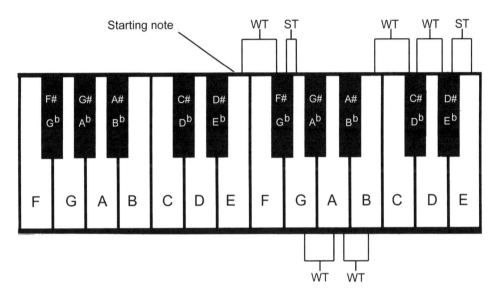

Figure 1.12a.   *e-melodic minor scale (ascending)*

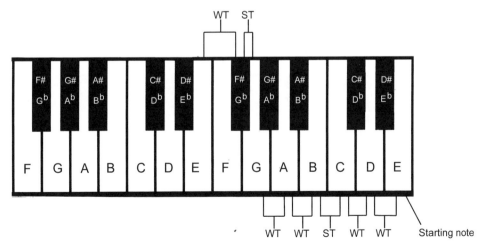

Figure 1.12b.   *e-melodic minor scale (descending)*

In any key, scale degree notes have specific names. The first scale degree is the *tonic*, the second is the *supertonic*, the third is the *mediant*, the fourth is the *subdominant*, the fifth is the *dominant*, and the sixth is the *submediant*.

In a discussion of scales and modality, special notice should be taken of the mediant. This third scale degree is important because it establishes either major or minor mode.

The seventh degree of major and the various minor scales is "variable." In some cases, the distance below tonic is a semitone, while in others it is a whole tone. In the major mode, the seventh scale degree is the *leading tone* because it is a mere semitone from the tonic, which gives it a feeling of leading to or resolving to the tonic. The same is true with the harmonic minor and the ascending melodic scales. In the natural and the *descending melodic* scales, the seventh scale degree is the *subtonic* because this *now-lowered* tone is a whole tone below the tonic. Finally, the eighth scale degree is the *octave* or *high tonic* (figures 1.13a and 1.13b).

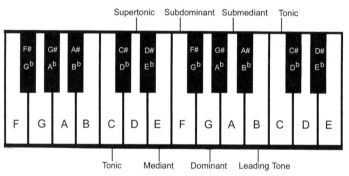

Figure 1.13a. *Major scale with scale degree names*

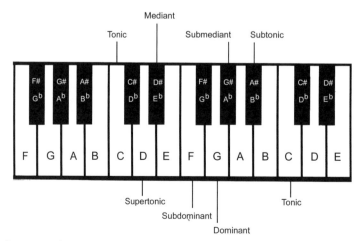

Figure 1.13b. *Natural minor scale with scale degree names*

When any two pitches sound consecutively or simultaneously, the distance between each is an *interval*. Intervals are defined by two components—size and quality. They can be perceived aurally as well as visually. In order to determine interval *size* visually, start with the bottom note and count lines and spaces to the upper note. Be sure to count both the starting and ending notes. For example, on the staff below, starting on C and ending on the same C is a unison. Starting on C and ending on D, the interval is a second. The distance from C to E is a third, and so forth. An interval of an eighth is an octave (figures 1.14 and 1.15).

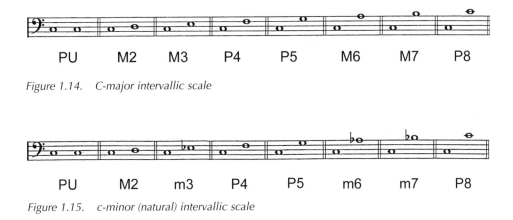

Figure 1.14.   C-major intervallic scale

Figure 1.15.   c-minor (natural) intervallic scale

Notice on the major and minor scales above that the thirds, sixths, and sevenths would sound different, depending upon the mode. In addition, the specific distance (number of semitones or whole tones) has changed. These variances represent the interval *quality*. We define these intervallic qualities as major, minor, *perfect*, *diminished*, and *augmented*. Perfect intervals are intervals that are the same in major and minor modes. These intervals are typically described as "open" and "hollow."

The interval size and qualities from the tonic are labeled on the C-major scale above (figure 1.14). Notice that the unison, fourth, fifth, and octave are perfect (P), and the second, third, sixth, and seventh intervals are major (M).

The interval size and qualities (again from the tonic) are labeled on the c-natural minor scale above (figure 1.15). As is the case in a major mode, the unison, fourth, fifth, and octave remain perfect. Likewise, the second remains major. However, the third, sixth, and seventh intervals are now minor (m). Considering the intervals of the third, sixth, and seventh in both scales, the major interval is "bigger," while the minor interval is "smaller."

The word "augment" means to increase, and "diminish" means to decrease. When a perfect fourth is augmented or a perfect fifth is diminished they create a *tritone*. A tritone is three whole tones (figure 1.16).

Figure 1.16.   Augmented fourth or diminished fifth

An augmented fourth and a diminished fifth sound the same. *Enharmonic* equivalents are pitches that sound the same but are written differently. For example, a D-sharp and an E-flat are the same pitch, but with different spellings. The same is true of F and E-sharp. Actually, each tone can be written in one of two or three ways (figure 1.17).

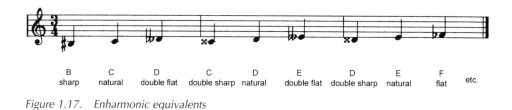

Figure 1.17.   Enharmonic equivalents

In the context of a major or minor scale, the tritone does not appear as an interval above or below the tonic, but it can be embedded within the scale. For example, in a major scale, the distance between the subdominant and the leading tone is an augmented fourth (figure 1.18).

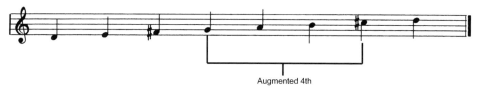

Figure 1.18.   Augmented fourth in a major scale

For each scale, *key* is the means of identifying the tonal center (*root* or tonic) and mode. Sharps and flats indicate the *key signature* at the beginning of a composition. Key signature can change at any point as *modulations* (or shifts in tonal center) between keys occur. As already stated, key signatures may contain accidentals.

The order of sharps in a key signature is always the same (figure 1.19).

Figure 1.19. Order of sharps

The order of flats in a key signature is always the same (figure 1.20).

Figure 1.20. Order of flats

The number of accidentals in a key signature identifies the key's tonic. For example, one sharp (F♯) is the key signature for G-major. So, if one begins a scale on G and then follows the formula for a *major* scale, one finds that the leading tone is F-sharp. The major key signatures follow (figure 1.21).

Figure 1.21. Major key signatures

The *circle of fifths* is another system of key identification. It considers the increasing number of sharps or flats in the signatures. Starting with C-major (no sharps or flats) and moving clockwise by ascending fifths, one reaches G-major (one sharp). Ascending a fifth again, one reaches D-major (two sharps), and so on. After twelve steps, one returns to C-major. Likewise, starting with C-major (no sharps or flats) and moving counterclockwise by descending fifths, one reaches F-major (one flat). Descending a fifth again, one reaches B-flat major (two flats), and so on. After twelve steps, one returns again to C-major (figure 1.22).

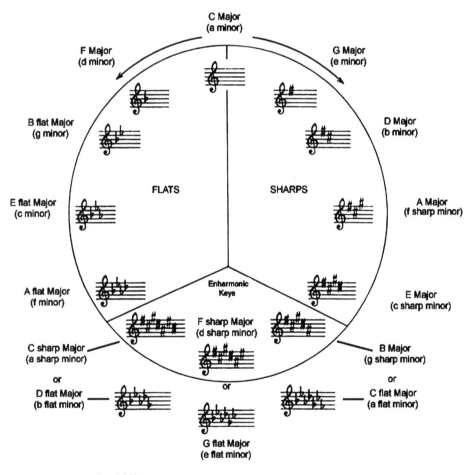

Figure 1.22.   Circle of fifths

The astute student will memorize key signatures. As an aid in retention, the following tips may prove helpful.

To determine a major key in a key signature containing sharps, simply name the sharp farthest to the right in the key signature and go up one letter name. Then add the word "major" and that is the key. For example, in the key of E-major, the sharp in the key signature that is the farthest right is D. Therefore, if one goes up one letter name, one arrives at E, hence E-major.

To determine a major key in the key signature containing flats, simply name the flat second from the right in the key signature and add the word "flat" to its letter name. Then add the word "major" and that is the key. For example, the key signature of E♭-major shows an E♭ as the second from the right.

The exception to the system above is that if there is only one flat in the key signature, the key is F-major. If there are no flats or sharps in the key signature, the key is C-major.

Key signatures apply to minor scales as well. Each major key has a *relative* natural minor which is down, intervalically, a minor third. That is, C-major's relative minor key is A-minor. Therefore, the key of A-natural minor has the same key signature as C-major; it simply begins on A rather than on C. Using that key signature, one merely adds the appropriate accidentals to construct the harmonic and melodic variations of the minor mode (figure 1.23).

Figure 1.23.   C-major scale and its relative minor

In "King Herod's Song" from *Jesus Christ Superstar*, Andrew Lloyd Webber begins the song in f-sharp minor. At measure 9, the relative key, A-major, is established and evident in the shift from a darker, ominous quality to one that is brighter (figure 1.24).

Figure 1.24. "King Herod's Song," mm. 1–4 and 9–16, relative key relationship

Note that in measures 15 and 16, A-major is reinforced with the descending major scale in the melody.

One other key relationship is the *parallel*. Parallel key relationships have the same tonic but different key signatures and notes. For example, d-minor is the parallel minor of D-major.

Notice on the scales below, C-major has no sharps or flats in the key signature (figure 1.25a). A c-minor scale has three flats (figure 1.25b), reflected in the key signature (figure 1.25c). If those three flats are translated into the key signature for the appropriate major key, it would be E-flat major (figure 1.25d). Note that E-flat major's relative minor, then, is c-minor (an interval of a third below).

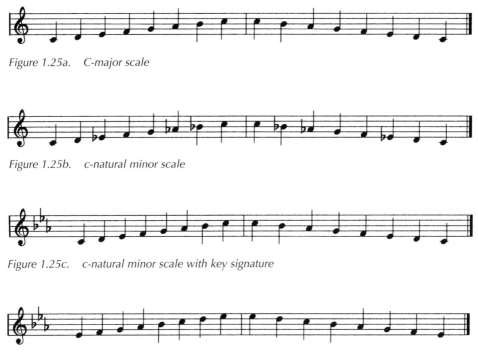

Figure 1.25a.   C-major scale

Figure 1.25b.   c-natural minor scale

Figure 1.25c.   c-natural minor scale with key signature

Figure 1.25d.   E-flat major scale with key signature

Composers can use the device of *mutation*, or changing mode to a parallel major or minor, without altering the key. The song "Far from the Home I Love" from *Fiddler on the Roof* provides a clear example. The song begins in the key of c-minor. At measure 12, through the use of accidentals and an ascending C-major scale in the accompaniment, the parallel major key is established to reinforce the happy recollection (figure 1.26).

Another example of mutation appears in "I Enjoy Being a Girl," from *Flower Drum Song*. In this instance, the key shift is from D-major to d-minor (figure 1.27).

The musical theatre examples quoted thus far are evidence of the potency of melody as a guide to the listener and to the performer. When one considers harmony as an extension of the melodic expression, an infinite number of musical possibilities unfold. Harmony can reinforce emotion and dramatic action, and sustain a mood.

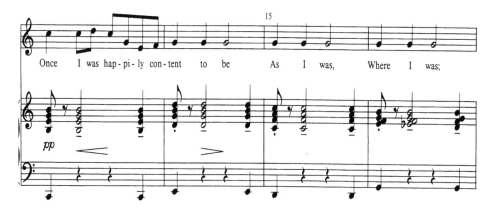

Figure 1.26.   "Far from the Home I Love," mm. 5–16, mutation

Figure 1.27. "*I Enjoy Being a Girl,*" *mm. 53–63, mutation*

Harmony

Harmony refers to the simultaneous sounding of two or more pitches or tones. This coupling of tones begins to characterize sound just as a coupling of people begins to characterize a conversation or relationship. Primarily, harmony references music vertically, while melody suggests a linear or horizontal orientation.

Harmony is organized in many ways, but the underlying principle behind harmony is *tertian*—chords built in thirds. A *triad* is a three-note chord that contains a root or starting note, the note a third above the root, and a note a fifth above the root. Four examples of triads built on C appear below (figures 1.28a, 1.28b, 1.28c, and 1.28d).

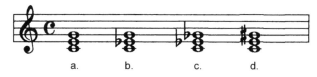

Figure 1.28a, Figure 1.28b, Figure 1.28c, Figure 1.28d.   Four triads built on C

The third and the fifth notes of the triad indicate mode. When the distance between the root and fifth of a triad is perfect, the modality is either major or minor. In the example above, figures 1.28a and 1.28b are major and minor triads. The determining factor in this case is the interval between the root and the third above. When the distance between the root and the fifth is reduced by one semitone, it is a *diminished* triad. In this case, there will always be an interval of a *minor* third between the root of the chord and the third (figure 1.28c). Conversely, when the interval of the fifth is raised by one semitone, it is an *augmented* triad and will always contain a *major* third between the root and third (figure 1.28d).

Just as the mode of intervals is indicated by upper- or lowercase letters, the mode of triads is indicated by upper- or lowercase Roman numerals.

The triadic scale in a major key features major triads on the tonic, fourth, and fifth scale degrees. They are identified by the Roman numerals I, IV, and V. The triadic scale in a minor key features minor triads on the second, third, and sixth scale degrees. They are identified by the lowercase Roman numerals ii, iii, and vi. A diminished triad (lowered by one semitone) is found on the seventh scale degree in a major scale. It is thus identified by a lowercase Roman number vii followed by a °, as in vii° (figure 1.29).

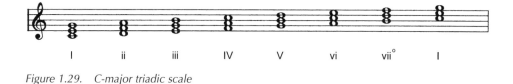

I   ii   iii   IV   V   vi   vii°   I

Figure 1.29.   C-major triadic scale

The triadic scale above is in the key of C-major, evidenced by the fact that there are no accidentals in the key signature and it begins and ends on c. The triadic scale for a-minor (the relative minor of C-major) follows (figure 1.30).

Notice that the a-natural minor triadic scale features major chords constructed on the third, sixth, and seventh scale degrees. They are identified by the Roman numerals III, VI, and VII. Chords constructed on the tonic,

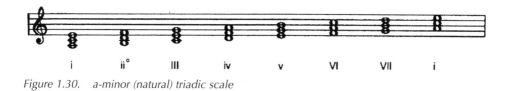

Figure 1.30. *a-minor (natural) triadic scale*

fourth, and fifth scale degrees are minor and are identified by the lower-case Roman numerals i, iv, and v. The triad built on the second scale degree is diminished and is identified by a lowercase Roman number ii followed by a °, as in ii°. Notice that the augmented triad is not present in the major or the natural minor scale. It *does* appear, however, on iii in both harmonic and ascending melodic minor scales. It is a unique and versatile compositional device that adds expressive variety to music. Because it is a triad constructed of stacked major thirds, the notation is an uppercase Roman numeral followed by a +, as in III+ (figure 1.31).

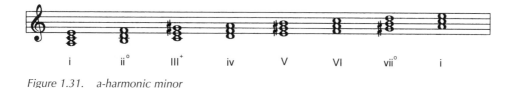

Figure 1.31. *a-harmonic minor*

The introduction to "Chop Suey" is in the key of C-major and the treble clef features a sequence of parallel triads that include major, minor, and diminished sonorities (figure 1.32).

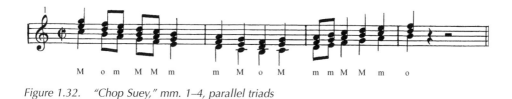

Figure 1.32. *"Chop Suey," mm. 1–4, parallel triads*

Thus far, we have considered triads in *root position* only—that is, stacked thirds with the root on the bottom. There are two alternative voicings for triads that, by virtue of the rearranged tones, can alter the feeling of tonal stability. By taking the root of the triad and placing it an octave above, the *third* of the triad is now the bottom note. As such, the notes are no longer arranged by stacked thirds. The upper notes are now a sixth and a third above the bottom note. This is notated with a subscript $_6$ next to the

Roman numeral and is in *first inversion*. Because triads are inherently built on a system of thirds, it is not necessary to notate the third that exists between the bottom two notes (figure 1.33).

Figure 1.33.   *Root and first inversion triads*

Triads in *second inversion* feature the third of the triad now an octave higher, leaving the fifth of the triad as the bottom note. The resulting intervals above that fifth are now a sixth and a fourth. In this case, the subscript $^6_4$ is notated (figure 1.34).

Figure 1.34.   *Root position, first and second inversion triads*

A shift between root-position and second-inversion triads is captured in "Love, Look Away," from *Flower Drum Song*. Notice that, in measures 5–7, the melody outlines two consecutive minor triads—g-minor and f-minor, and then a diminished triad in measure 9. In the accompaniment of measure 6, Richard Rodgers has spelled a sequence of parallel triads in first inversion (in this case, major, minor, major, minor; see figure 1.35).

Figure 1.35.   *"Love, Look Away," mm. 5–9, parallel triads*

Inversions of triads do not change the mode, so upper- and lowercase notation remains consistent. What changes, however, is the perceived stability and coloring of the chord. Depending upon the context, a first-inversion triad may sound less "final" than a root-position triad. Similarly, in a second-inversion chord, burying the root within the chord obscures the feeling of stability or finality. Additionally, with the exposed third on the top, the *mode* is much more apparent, and it suggests harmonic or melodic movement.

In the introduction to this book, a parallel was drawn between a playwright's use of literal language and a composer's use of musical language. If chords form "words," then musical phrases form "sentences" that must be punctuated.

A *cadence* is a progression of two or more chords at the end of a musical phrase. In a way, a cadence functions as a "period," an "exclamation point," or a "comma." The cadence V to I is an *authentic* cadence. Because the authentic cadence features the dominant and tonic scale degrees, it represents the *strongest* (and most common) musical punctuation. The cadence IV to I is a *plagal* cadence and is the second-most-common cadential pattern in Western music. A *deceptive* cadence is one in which the progression from the dominant chord *denies* resolution to the tonic, and replaces it with resolution to iii or to vi. A *half cadence* is one in which the final chord is a V (figures 1.36a, 1.36b, 1.36c, and 1.36d).

C: Authentic   Plagal   Deceptive   Half

Figure 1.36a, Figure 1.36b, Figure 1.36c, Figure 1.36d.   Cadences

Harmony is not limited to triadic structures. Stated simply, it is possible to stack additional thirds above the triad. The most common use of this extended tertian harmony is the addition of the seventh. Added ninths, elevenths, and thirteenths are *higher-order tertian* (H.O.T.) chords and, like seventh chords, provide richer harmonic color and character.

Remember that the relationship between the root and third of a triad determines major or minor modality. The relationship of root to fifth characterizes perfect, augmented, and diminished qualities. Because of the additional third, seventh chords have a two-name moniker. The first name refers to the root-third (major or minor) relationship. The second name refers to the root-seventh relationship. Therefore, many seventh chords are either *Major-Major* (MM), *Major-minor* (Mm), *minor-minor* (mm), or *minor-Major* (mM). Additionally, in the case of a root-fifth relationship that is diminished, a seventh chord with a minor seventh is called *half diminished* and a seventh chord with a diminished fifth and a diminished seventh is called (fully) *diminished* (figure 1.37).

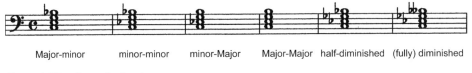

Figure 1.37.   Seventh chords

Stephen Sondheim exploits a variety of higher-order tertian chords in the accompaniment to "Side by Side by Side," from *Company*, possibly in order to express a disconnect between what is being sung and what Bobby, the main character, is feeling. In measure 29, there is a half-diminished seventh chord. Minor-Major seventh chords appear in measures 31 and 37. Measures 63 and 64 feature a Major-minor ninth followed by a minor-minor ninth chord (figure 1.38).

Figure 1.38.   "Side by Side by Side," mm. 29–32, 37–40, 63–64, examples of seventh and ninth chords

Figure 1.38. (Continued).

It is important to note that vertical construction of triads and chords is not the only manner in which higher-order tertian harmony can be utilized. Sometimes, it is the accumulation of chord tones shared between melody and accompaniment and developed over the course of a number of beats that "implies" the ninth, eleventh, and thirteenth harmony. A classic example is in Sondheim's "Being Alive," from *Company*. For instance, in the example below, notice that the accompaniment of the whole of measure 20 spells an (incomplete) thirteenth chord—e-flat, g, b-flat, (d), f, a-flat, c. Later in the same song, as the drama builds to a climax, this higher-order sensibility is intensified as Sondheim now thickens the texture of the accompaniment and places the thirteenth of the chord in the melody—b, (d-sharp), (f-sharp), a, c-sharp, e, g-sharp (figure 1.39).

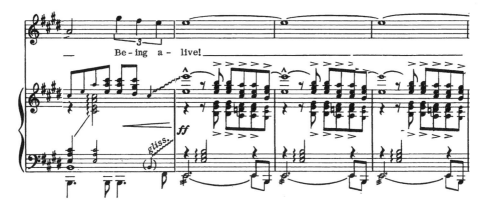

Figure 1.39. "Being Alive," mm. 20–21, 131–136

Figure 1.39.   (Continued).

Exposition, rise in conflict, climax, and resolution tie musical composition to principles of storytelling. Harmony can exist on two levels: vertical and horizontal. Much of the discussion above addresses harmony in a stacked or vertical context. In this way, harmony is creating the "words" of music. Perhaps harmony's greatest function, however, is its ability to provide forward movement, thereby establishing the "thought" or "sentence" of music. The combination of harmony and melody, traveling forward in time, creates a complete statement that is a *harmonic progression*. Harmonic progressions often operate on a basic level within the key—for example, a tonic moving toward a dominant and eventually returning to tonic.

Functional harmony is the prevailing harmonic language of Western music and as such is the predominant harmonic idiom of American popular music. Since the music of the American musical theatre began firmly rooted as *the* popular music of the country, it logically adopted this functional harmonic vocabulary in a majority of its repertoire. Whether chords associate with melody or interact with other chords, functional harmony results in an emotional impulse that has proven nearly universal. These impulses serve as powerful cues for performers and listeners alike. Functional harmony establishes an emotional current that directs music to an emotional destination. These "progressions" of chords create syntax.

A tonic chord, for example, can move to any other chord in a key, and that initial movement may suggest subsequent progressions (figure 1.40).

Figure 1.40.   Tonic chord progressions

In general terms, a dominant chord moves with ease to a tonic or to a submediant (in which case the aforementioned deceptive cadence results). A dominant can also move with ease to a subdominant chord (figure 1.41).

C: V — I   V — vi   V — IV — I

Figure 1.41.   Dominant chord progressions

A subdominant chord typically progresses to a dominant, submediant, supertonic, or tonic chord (in the latter case, a plagal cadence results; see figure 1.42).

C: V — I   V — vi   V — IV — I

Figure 1.42.   Subdominant chord progressions

A supertonic chord generally moves to a dominant or to a tonic chord (figure 1.43).

C: ii — V   ii — I

Figure 1.43.   Supertonic chord progressions

A submediant leads to the subdominant or to the supertonic chord (figure 1.44).

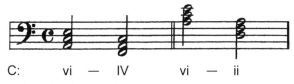

C: vi — IV   vi — ii

Figure 1.44.   Submediant chord progressions

The same rules that govern two-chord progressions can be applied to multichord progressions (figure 1.45).

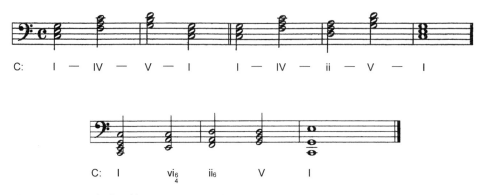

Figure 1.45. Multichord harmonic progressions

In the excerpt below, composer Andrew Lloyd Webber uses a traditional chord progression to accompany the melody of "I Don't Know How to Love Him." Webber's chords progress from tonic to some other sonority and then back again. Furthermore, those additional sonorities are closely related (figure 1.46).

Figure 1.46. "I Don't Know How to Love Him," mm. 1–8, traditional chord progression

move _____ him, I've been changed   yes real-ly   changed   In these

I⁶₄   V   I₆   vi₆   V   I   vi₆   (V⁴₂)

Figure 1.46.   (Continued).

A basic four-measure chord progression appears below. Note that the melody constructed above it consists of tones that are derived from the supporting accompaniment. That is, the melodic tones above the tonic chord (I) are C, E, or G. When the harmony changes to the subdominant (IV), the melody consists of F, A, or C, etc. (figure 1.47).

C: I   V   ii   IV   vi   V   iii   IV   V   I

Figure 1.47.   Simple chord-tone melody with accompaniment

The song "Can't Help Lovin' Dat Man," from the classic musical *Show Boat*, provides a clear illustration of another traditional chord progression supported by a chord-tone melody (figure 1.48).

Fish got to swim_ and birds got to fly,—   I got to love_ one

E♭:   I   vi   ii⁷   V⁷   I   vi

Figure 1.48.   "Can't Help Lovin' Dat Man," mm. 1–4, traditional harmony with chord-tone melody

IV

Figure 1.48. (Continued).

Music's richness lies in the combination of melody and harmony. It is possible to enhance melodic and harmonic vocabulary with the addition of *nonharmonic tones*. A nonharmonic tone is foreign to the momentary harmony, and its tonal function is to expand the musical context. The example below is identical to the example above except for the addition of nonharmonic tones that provide variety and interest (figure 1.49).

C: I   V   ii   IV   vi   V   iii   IV   V   I

Figure 1.49.   Simple melody with nonharmonic tones and accompaniment

Nonharmonic tones fall into two basic categories—rhythmically weak and rhythmically strong—and each one is identified easily by certain characteristics. A *passing tone* occurs between two stepwise notes on an unaccented beat and can move in any direction. It can be either diatonic (figure 1.50a) or chromatic (figure 1.50b).

Figure 1.50a.   Diatonic passing tone

Figure 1.50b.   Chromatic passing tone

Jason Robert Brown's "Christmas Lullaby" from *Songs for a New World* and Jerry Bock and Sheldon Harnick's "Matchmaker, Matchmaker" from *Fiddler on the Roof* illustrate two different treatments of the use of passing tones (figures 1.51a and 1.51b). In the case of "Christmas Lullaby," *accented* passing tones serve as an *ornament* on a monosyllabic word. In "Matchmaker, Matchmaker," the *unaccented* passing tones are used *melodically*.

Figure 1.51a.   "Christmas Lullaby," mm. 28–31, diatonic passing tone

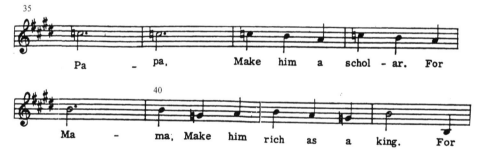

Figure 1.51b.   "Matchmaker, Matchmaker," mm. 35–42, diatonic passing tones

An *anticipation* is a tone that foreshadows an approaching harmonic change. In the example below, note that the nonharmonic tone *becomes* harmonic upon resolution (figure 1.52).

Figure 1.52.   Anticipation

In "Christmas Lullaby," the anticipation is not used cadentially but as part of the harmonic progression (figure 1.53).

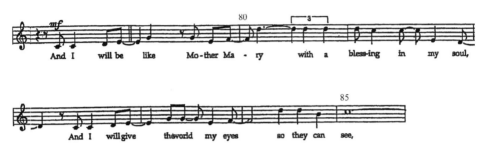

Figure 1.53.   "Christmas Lullaby," mm. 78–85, anticipations

Conversely, a *retardation* forestalls, by melodic extension, a complete harmonic resolution. In the example below, note that the nonharmonic tone *delays* the full resolution to the V chord (figure 1.54).

Figure 1.54.   Retardation

An *échappée* is a nonharmonic tone that "escapes" resolution in the "wrong" direction by step and then resolves by a leap of a third in the "right" direction (figure 1.55).

Figure 1.55.   Échappée

Jerome Kern used an échappée to great effect in "You Are Love," from *Show Boat*. By ascending to the G, Kern seems to underscore the importance of the verb in the lyric (figure 1.56).

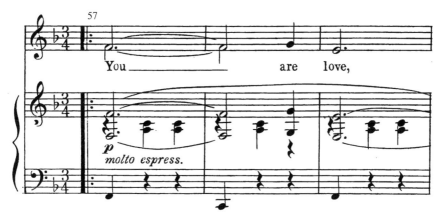

Figure 1.56. *"You Are Love," mm. 57–59, échappée*

A *cambiata* is a nonharmonic tone that *overshoots* in the direction of resolution by a third and resolves by step in the opposite direction as the harmony is maintained (figure 1.57).

Figure 1.57. *Cambiata*

A cambiata appears in measure 18 in Stephen Sondheim's song "Sorry-Grateful," from *Company* (figure 1.58).

Figure 1.58. *"Sorry-Grateful," mm. 17–18, cambiata*

Neighbor tones are melodic ornaments that move stepwise (diatonically or chromatically) away from and back to a given harmonic tone (figure 1.59).

Figure 1.59.   Neighbor tones

Two examples of neighbor tones appear below. The first, a lower-neighbor tone, is in "I Enjoy Being a Girl," from Rodgers and Hammerstein's *Flower Drum Song* (figure 1.60a.) An upper-neighbor tone appears in Jason Robert Brown's "I'm Not Afraid," from *Songs for a New World* (figure 1.60b).

Figure 1.60a.   "I Enjoy Being a Girl," mm. 28–31, lower-neighbor tone

Figure 1.60b.   "I'm Not Afraid," mm. 13–14, upper-neighbor tone

There are two rhythmically strong nonharmonic tones: the appoggiatura and the suspension. The *appoggiatura* sounds on a strong beat and then resolves afterwards. The examples below show various appoggiatura configurations of a D-major triad (figure 1.61).

Figure 1.61.   Appoggiaturas

Turning to "Can't Help Lovin' Dat Man" again, Kern uses the appoggiatura on beat 3 in measure 20 (figure 1.62).

The example below features a "prepared appoggiatura" with the non-harmonic tone sounding in the preceding chord (figure 1.63).

Figure 1.62. "Can't Help Lovin' Dat Man," mm. 19–22, appoggiatura

Figure 1.63. Prepared appoggiatura

A prepared appoggiatura appears in measures 3–9 of "Matchmaker, Matchmaker" (figure 1.64).

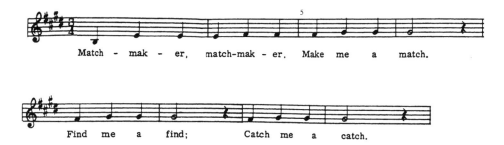

Figure 1.64. "Matchmaker, Matchmaker," mm. 3–9, prepared appoggiatura

A suspension is the same as a prepared appoggiatura with the exception that the dissonant note is repeated or tied from the chord preceding (figure 1.65).

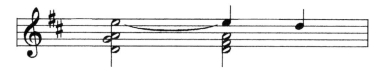

Figure 1.65. Suspension

A suspension in measure 8 in the inner voice of the accompaniment of "Love, Look Away" adds harmonic interest (figure 1.66).

Figure 1.66. *"Love, Look Away," mm. 5–8, suspension*

Nonharmonic expression is not limited to melody. Harmony can be extended by the use of nonharmonic tones, thereby revealing an array of musical possibilities. Just as higher-order tertian structures provide the opportunity for musical interest and variety, so music can "travel" away from its tonal center through a reconceptualization of the dominant chord. Every scale degree has a fifth above and below it. Building a triad on the fifth of any scale degree adds a layer of harmonic context. This emphasis of the dominant scale degree echoes the notion of the circle of fifths as a way of considering harmonic relationship.

In the example below, note the tonic triad in C-major. Next to it is a major triad built on the dominant scale degree (G–B–D). What follows is a major triad built on the D, the fifth of the dominant triad. The major triad built upon this D is D–F#–A. The presence of the F# clearly moves away from C-major. It cannot be analyzed as a ii chord in C-major, for that would have to be a *minor* triad. This major chord functions as the dominant of the dominant, or V of V in C-major (figure 1.67).

Figure 1.67. *Example of the V/V chord in C-major*

Likewise, this concept can be applied to any scale degree within the key. One could build the triad on the second degree, note its fifth, the A, and build a major triad on that A, resulting in a chord spelled as A–C#–E. This is the V of ii in the key of C-major. This approach to harmony allows a composer to move away from a tonal center without a formal modulation. It allows for more complex musical expression and can facilitate formal modulation. *Modulation* takes place when a new dominant-tonic relationship is firmly established.

Another compositional device that adds *more* harmonic tension than a plain dominant triad, particularly when a change in key in imminent, is the dominant seventh chord. It functions as the dominant triad does, but with a more urgent tendency to progress to the tonic (figure 1.68).

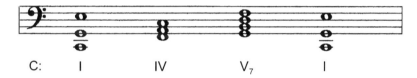

Figure 1.68.   Example of V7 chord in the key of C-major

Just as harmonic progression provides forward movement of musical thought, modulation from one key to another can add an additional layer of intensity, urgency, and interest to the musical journey. The heightened emotion inherent in theatre music occurs as the character moves through conflict toward resolution. Modulation can be the composer's nonverbal contribution to that journey. It can occur in several ways. The transition from an established key to a destination key can be smooth or abrupt. Modulation relies upon cadential patterns or a new key signature to be complete.

Two keys may share common chords. For example, a V in C-major is also a I in G-major. When one chord is a bridge from an established key to a destination key, a *common chord* modulation has occurred. The common chord acts as a "pivot," facilitating the movement between the keys.

"A New World" from Jason Robert Brown's *Songs for a New World* provides an interesting example of a strong modulation from E-flat major to B-flat major. Note that the E-flat major chord in measure 68 (the tonic or I) is also a IV in the destination key of B-flat major. The addition of an F pedal point in the bass (dominant reinforcement of the new key) strengthens the modulation. A *pedal point* is a tone that is sustained in the bass as harmony above changes (figure 1.69).

Figure 1.69. "A New World," mm. 58–72, common-chord modulation

A second type of modulation, *enharmonic modulation*, occurs when one chord in the established key is spelled enharmonically in the destination key. In measure 60 from Stephen Sondheim's "Losing My Mind" from Follies, the chord is spelled G-flat, B-flat, D-flat, E-natural (a subtonic harmony in the original key) on beat 1. Its repetition on the third beat is spelled f-sharp, a-sharp, c-sharp, e—the dominant-seventh chord of B-major, the destination key (figure 1.70).

Figure 1.70.   "Losing My Mind," mm. 59–61, enharmonic modulation

From the earliest days of American musical theatre, excitement has been generated by one of the most frequently encountered shifts in tonal center that exists: sudden upward modulation by half step without the utilization of a common chord. Used to great effect in musical theatre literature, it is the *direct* or *abrupt modulation*. This type of modulation features a cadence in the established key that is followed by the next phrase in a new key, often a semitone or whole tone higher. This modulation has the effect of "shifting without a clutch," because the musical energy parallels a sudden or urgent rise in emotional intensity.

A classic example of the power of an abrupt modulation can be found in Stephen Sondheim's "Being Alive" from *Company*. To build intensity toward a musical and dramatic climax, the song ascends abruptly from E-flat major to E-major with no preparation (figure 1.71).

Figure 1.71.   "Being Alive," mm. 73–77, abrupt modulation

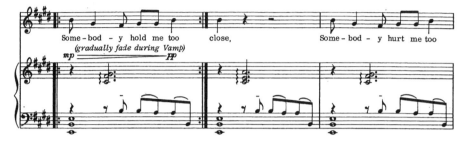

Figure 1.71.   (Continued).

Sometimes, a piece of music can start and end in a particular key but will temporarily modulate to a new key *without* formally altering the key signature. The chorus of "Ol' Man River," from *Show Boat*, by Jerome Kern, is a classic example. In the excerpt below, the chorus begins and ends in the key of C-major. The addition of accidentals (F-sharp and D-sharp) moves the key of the bridge to e-minor without altering the key signature. The new key is established at the outset of the bridge, but the vacillation between I and V (e-minor, B-major) is in the accompaniment. This tonic-dominant relationship is reiterated further by the prominence of an A-natural in the melody, implying a dominant *seventh* context. The return to the original key is facilitated in measures 32 and 33. The e-minor chord serves as both i in the bridge and also iii in C-major, the return of the original key (figure 1.72).

Figure 1.72.   "Ol' Man River," mm. 15–34, temporary modulation

Modulation

e minor (temporary)

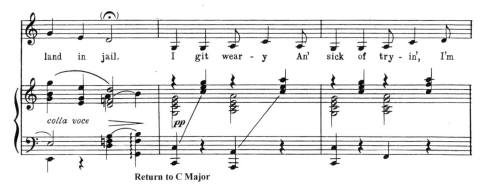

Return to C Major

Figure 1.72. (Continued).

A musical statement is not complete without a sense of movement. Rhythm achieves forward motion in music. Whether simple or complex, rhythm provides information that further defines character and dramatic situation.

Rhythm

Rhythm refers to the pattern established by unit duration. *Meter* is the regular recurrence of alternating stressed and unstressed beats or units. As such, notes that are combined to create rhythmic patterns vary in duration. Likewise, *rests*, or durations of silence, have varying values (figure 1.73).

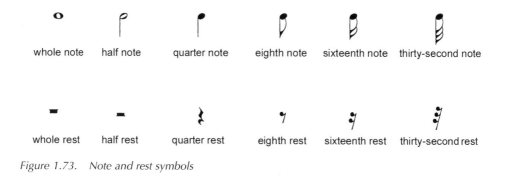

Figure 1.73.   Note and rest symbols

Dotting a note or rest adds half of its value to it.

Measures divide meter into regularly recurring divisions. Vertical lines on the staff, *bar lines*, indicate measures (also called bars).

A *time signature* typically appears at the beginning of every composition. It indicates the initiation of a new meter once the initial time signature has been established. The upper number in a time signature indicates the number of beats per measure. The lower number in a time signature indicates the type of note that receives one beat (figure 1.74).

Figure 1.74.   Staff with time signatures, bar lines, and rhythmic patterns

An exception to the rest notation explained above is that a *whole rest* also indicates an *entire measure* of silence regardless of the time signature. For instance, in $\frac{3}{4}$ time, an entire measure of rest would be notated with a whole rest rather than with a dotted half rest. Similarly, in $\frac{6}{8}$ time, a whole rest indicates an entire measure of silence rather than a dotted half rest (figure 1.75).

Figure 1.75.   Whole rest in various metrical settings

The time signature $\frac{4}{4}$ is known also as *"common* time" as shown below (figure 1.76).

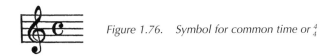

Figure 1.76.   Symbol for common time or $\frac{4}{4}$

In *cut time* ($\frac{2}{2}$), the half note, rather than the quarter note, receives the beat. The symbol for cut time is shown below (figure 1.77).

Figure 1.77.   Symbol for cut time

Rhythmic patterns having two beats or multiples thereof ($\frac{2}{2}$, $\frac{2}{4}$, $\frac{4}{4}$) are in *duple meter*. Likewise, rhythmic patterns having three beats ($\frac{3}{4}$, $\frac{3}{8}$) are in *triple meter*. In $\frac{2}{2}$ and $\frac{2}{4}$ time, the first beat (*downbeat*) is accented, while the last beat (*upbeat*) is unaccented. In $\frac{3}{4}$ and $\frac{3}{8}$ time, the first beat is accented, while the second and third beats are unaccented. In $\frac{4}{4}$ time, there are two accents felt—the first and third beats.

Tempo, or relative speed of rhythm, can affect the way meter is perceived. For example, a quick $\frac{3}{4}$ or $\frac{3}{8}$ meter may be perceived in one predominant pulse per measure. Likewise, $\frac{6}{8}$ may be perceived as having two predominant accents, on beats 1 and 4, while $\frac{6}{8}$ can be subdivided into three, with predominant accents on beats 1, 4, and 7, thereby classifying it as a form of triple meter. And $\frac{12}{8}$ can be subdivided into four.

Form

The form of musical theatre literature can be as varied as any other musical genre. But, because the roots of musical theatre literature are found in popular music, whose forms are necessarily short, there are general structural components common to most of the repertoire from the late nineteenth century onward.

Most musical theatre songs begin with an instrumental *introduction*. The introduction can be of varying length. It can be as simple as a single note that provides a starting pitch for the singer or as complex as a multi-measure cell that introduces a musical motif.

The introduction typically is followed by the *verse*. The text of the verse tends to be expository, that is, it provides key background information, and, therefore, the music serves as transition from speech into singing. As such, it is performed generally in a more rhythmically free manner that reflects speechlike patterns.

It is usually the *chorus* that is the most memorable section of a musical theatre song. The text brings specificity to the notions expressed in the verse. Because the focus of the lyric is narrow, the musical structure is more concise. A typical chorus is built of four eight-measure phrases. For the purpose of analysis, each phrase is identified by a letter. Sections that are closely related are assigned the same letter, while contrasting sections receive other letters. The most frequently found form is AABA, in which the A sections are exact or near-repeats of each other. The B, also called the *bridge* or *release*, features contrasting music, often in a relative or parallel key. The text of the bridge provides reflection and prepares the climactic return of the final A section. Other common song forms include ABA, ABAB, and ABACA (*rondo* form).

The end of a song can be extended by either a *coda*, a short variation serving as a finishing theme, or a *rideout*, which is an instrumental "tag" that punctuates the song.

These patterns, all of which feature some form of musical repetition, are known as *strophic* structures.

Many musical theatre songs written in these compact forms feature additional or new lyrics and repeat the chorus. The repetition that characterizes the strophic form has served an important role in the development and popularity of the musical theatre song. Nowadays, it is not uncommon for audience members to be familiar with the songs prior to seeing the live production of a new musical. But in years past, before records, tapes, CDs, and iPods, composers and publishers relied upon word of mouth as a primary means to market their product. Therefore, if the musical material was repeated enough in one song and the song reprised numerous times throughout the evening, audience members would leave the theatre humming the tunes. This increased the likelihood that they would purchase the sheet music. Tin Pan Alley blossomed and thrived on this marketing strategy since, at that time, the piano was a prominent part of the American culture. The piano parlor was the social center of neighborhood life. Neighbors and friends would gather around the piano to sing the newest Broadway hit, thereby ensuring a wider audience for the songs. In those days before radio, television, and the recording industry, this was the way music was popularized and, unlike today, the popular music of the day was the music of the stage. Compact musical forms are less necessary in the modern musical theatre. *Through-composed* songs, extended songs written with no sectional repetition, are becoming more and more prevalent as a result of today's audiences' ability to digest more complex compositions.

This fundamental exploration of the mechanics of music theory is little more than the "what" and "where." The "how" is the real point of this text—How can an artist use what he or she knows of melody, harmony, and rhythm and parlay that into an informed and vital performance? The next part of this book is a series of essays created by the authors that can serve as a model demonstrating how to use the principles of music theory as a means of gaining deeper insight into musical dramatists' original intent.

2

Essays in Music Analysis

The late music scholar Edward T. Cone delivered a series of lectures in 1972 at the University of California, Berkeley. The substance of those lectures, printed in *The Composer's Voice*, addresses, as does much of Cone's other writing, the notion that rich possibilities for interpretation exist for performers of musical works if they consider analyzing music in a way that goes well beyond mere traditional (harmonic, melodic, and rhythmic) examination.[1] Cone encouraged music (and theatre) artists to delve into the worlds of play structure, dramatic personae, and, in the case of vocal music, text analysis, in order to create a vital live performance. Cone's ideas have been applied to great effect by many musicians whose orientation to analysis is through musical form and structure first.

Through the authors' teaching experience in an academic setting, they have discovered that when elements of music theory are incorporated into the *process* of song interpretation, the *product* is inevitably richer.

In spite of specific direction offered by *some* composers and lyricists, the burden of song interpretation and performance falls to the musical theatre practitioner. In order to meet these challenges, the authors invite musical theatre artists to bring as much imagination and insight to the process of music analysis as they would to script analysis. In so doing, they benefit by infusing their typical dramatic or textual song analysis with elements of music theory.

Through the essays that follow, the authors offer models that illustrate approaches to song interpretation.

Protest and Resignation: Hammerstein and Kern's Anthem for the Ages

Jerome Kern is one of the American musical theatre's greatest musical dramatists. His extensive body of work and his commitment to story and character rank him among the select few composers who have truly shaped the musical theatre art form. Not content to compose commercial "tunes" for the sake of entertainment, Kern, along with Oscar Hammerstein II, pioneered the move toward a musical play. In this format, music and dance are fully integrated so that all aspects combine into a seamless story. Their *Show Boat*, produced in 1927, demonstrated that the musical could address serious issues, that characters could evolve over a span of many years, and that music could play as important a role as the lyrics and the libretto in expressing character, plot, and theme.

The chorus to "Ol' Man River" is a classic example of Kern's mastery of musical storytelling. The song has become an angry anthem against oppression in general, and of racial oppression in particular. Oscar Hammerstein described it as a song of resignation with an implied protest. Hammerstein also admitted that the song was first created because the production needed a song to be sung "in one" or in front of the curtain so that scenery could be changed "in two" or behind the curtain.

In the song, Joe, an old slave, likens his plight to the Mississippi River; it just keeps "rollin' along." The song gently hints at the inequity, irony, and impermanence of life as Joe wonders about legacy. Kern used some basic and simple compositional ideas to capture these profound and universal notions.

Kern elected to set the song in the key of C-major. It was a wise choice. It is an easy key in which to play because of the absence of accidentals and the sonority of the key is open and simple.

Likewise, Kern also chose to set the song in common time, or $\frac{4}{4}$. This is the predominant meter for most Western music and is, therefore, highly accessible and uncomplicated. To have set the song in a less common meter or to have changed meter might have given the song more complexity than would be appropriate for the character.

Harmonically, Kern uses a traditional and functional harmonic vocabulary for most of the chorus. Study of the first major musical phrase (measures 1–8) reveals a harmonic progression consisting of tonic, subdominant, dominant, and mediant harmonies. This progression features a consistent return to tonic harmony with the vi and IV chords used to provide modal variety and II^7 and V^7 used for slightly more complex coloring.

The next major musical phrase (measures 9–16) uses a nearly identical harmonic progression with the addition of one simple but effective change in measure 12. Kern introduces a diminished tonic chord on beat 3. This chord provides emotional intensity. But Kern immediately returns to the harmonic progression he established in the first musical phrase as if to hint at Joe's deeper pain without allowing him to move too quickly into its full expression.

In the third musical phrase (measures 17–24), Kern moves the harmonic vocabulary in a new direction. As was mentioned earlier in this text, Kern, through the use of accidentals and the reliance upon the d-sharp and f-sharp, makes a temporary modulation into the key of e-minor. What is interesting to note is that, even within this new tonal center, Kern continues to rely upon the tonic, the dominant, and the sixth chords. So even though he temporary shifts the song into the minor mode, he continues to use the harmonic vocabulary that is closely aligned with that of the first two phrases of the chorus. It is also interesting to see that when Kern uses the sixth chord in the new key, he does so in a diminished form—the same c-diminished chord that he so specifically introduced in the second phrase at measure 12.

The fourth and final phrase of the chorus (measures 25–32) features a clear return to the material established in the first and second phrases. Kern simply changes measures 28–32 to allow for the climactic finish of the song as the melody rises to the high third and finally cadences on the upper tonic.

This use of a fairly traditional and accessible harmonic vocabulary, like Kern's choice of key and meter, helps draw the listener in to the "everyman" quality of the character and his quest for meaning. And it should also be noted that Kern relies heavily on chord tones for his melody throughout the chorus. This functional approach only solidifies the musical and emotional familiarity for the listener. The unfettered and uncomplicated nature of the music allows the listener to focus completely on Joe and his lot in life.

Because he was trying to characterize both the essence of a river and a man who is in the later stage of his life, Kern made great use of rhythm to help captures the sense of slow and careful reflection.

In the first phrase, Kern established a strong undercurrent of slow, open half-note movement in the left hand of the accompaniment. Not only does he use the half-note rhythm to give the piece a sense of tempo and physical weight, but he also notates that the half-note chords are to be rolled as opposed to sounded with one synchronous strike of the keys. Kern is clearly characterizing the "roll" of the water—its ebb and flow to and from and within its shores. This sensibility is nicely reinforced in the melody, which moves in a slow-slow-fast-slow rhythm in measure 1 and is repeated throughout most of the first and second phrases. This use of the quarter-quarter-eighth-quarter combination suggests a slow, steady movement that builds to a quick forward surge that is then suspended, almost hesitant. It is a simple expression that is perfect for an old man contemplating his station in life.

When Kern moves into the third phrase, the release, the primary rhythmic unit is the quarter note. The slow, fluid flow of the first two phrases is replaced by a regular, almost militant, articulation on each beat. This provides forward drive and urgency as the character sings, in monosyllabic words, about "sweat," "strain," "pain," and "jail." In this section, Joe quotes his master's orders, and the feelings about his position in life seem to rise ferociously toward the surface. This simple move to the persistent quarter note helps communicate this inner transformation. However, the transformation is unrealized. In the fourth phrase, Kern has Joe return to the slower and less angular rhythms that began the chorus, an indication that he is resigned to the reality of his condition.

However, as the melody begins its climactic rise up to the high tonic and beyond, to the third, there is an emotional crescendo that registers for both Joe and the listener. And in measure 30, Kern adjusts the rhythm slightly so that instead of the slow-slow-fast-slow pattern, he has Joe sing a slow-slow-fast-fast-slow pattern that denies the syncopation into beat 4 and firmly anchors the rhythmic articulation on each beat. Given that this change occurs in the climactic measure of the entire song as the melody reaches to the high third and moves to the resolution on the high tonic, this subtle rhythmic change suggests that while Joe knows his place, he has, perhaps, found comfort in his *choice* to believe that, like the river, he too will roll along.

Ol' Man River

Lyrics by Oscar Hammerstein II

Music by Jerome Kern

long. _____ He don't plant ta - ters, He

don't plant cot - ton An' dem dat plants em' Is soon for - got - ten, But

ol' man riv - er, He jes' keeps rol - lin' a - long.

You an' me, we sweat an' strain, Bod - y all ach - in' an' racked wid' pain.

Tote dat barge! Lift dat bale! Git a lit - tle drunk An' you

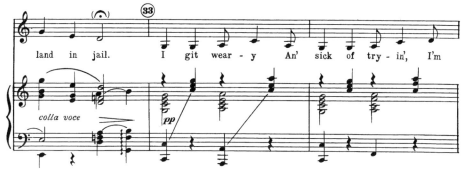

land in jail. I git wear - y An' sick of try - in', I'm

colla voce *pp*

tired of liv - in' An' skeered of dy - in'; But ol' man riv - er, He

f *f* (Hns)

jes' keeps rol - lin' a - long! _____

ff *fp*

Awake and Sing: "Just a Housewife"

Craig Carnelia's "Just a Housewife" from the musical *Working* charts the revelatory course of an American housewife, who, when asked about her job, at first responds that what she does is "nothing special." However, as she sings a list of the ordinary tasks that comprise her daily existence, she discovers an undercurrent of anger that eventually manifests itself into discovery and defense of her self-worth.

Carnelia uses key musical ideas to express the character's situation and emotional state. He wisely elects to keep the song simple and relies upon repetition to help communicate the essence of the monotony in her life.

Harmonically, the song relies upon two basic chords: I and V. In measures 5–12, Carnelia uses small building blocks or two-measure cells. In measure 5, the harmony consists of a tonic chord with a sustained supertonic (treble clef) that is followed by a descending pattern in the bass clef of measure 6 from the G-sharp (augmented fourth or tritone) to the F-sharp (mediant). This accompaniment pattern is repeated in measures 7 and 8 and appears throughout much of the song. The dominant harmony is first introduced in measures 9 and 10 as a V$_6$ chord in measure 9 with the aforementioned descending pattern repeating in measure 10. This two-measure motif is also repeated throughout the entire song.

The choice to use this limited harmonic vocabulary for the piece is inspired. It supports the simplicity of the character's daily life. The tonic and dominant harmonies are accessible, uncomplicated, and predictable, much like the housewife who is singing. The sustained supertonic layered on the tonic harmony (measure 5) provides a subtle dissonance that, along with the augmented fourth (measure 6), alludes that life beneath the surface may not be as simple and clean as we would be led to believe. It is also interesting to note that the G-sharp serves as an implied leading tone to the dominant scale degree when Carnelia moves to the dominant harmony in measures 9 and 10.

Carnelia also establishes another important relationship in these two opening motives. The tied tonic whole note in the bass clef in measures 5 and 6 acts as a pedal point, that is, a sustained but unarticulated pitch that tracks through the harmony under which it sounds. In measures 9 and 10, Carnelia continues this device with the tied C-sharp (the leading tone in the key of D-major) in the bass clef. By constructing the dominant harmony at measure 9 in first inversion, Carnelia establishes an important half-step relationship that will be used throughout the song as a device for modulation.

Because the character is moving from a position of passivity into one of defense, Carnelia chooses to abruptly change keys throughout the song. As already established, the song begins in D-major. At measure 45 the key raises one half step to E-flat major, only then to move back down to D-major at measure 61. At measure 81, the key again bumps up to E-flat major and then falls back down to D-major at measure 95. The song finishes in the key in which it began.

This constant movement up and down by half steps echoes the half-step relationship of the pedals Carnelia uses in measures 5–6 and 9–10. This vacillation away from and back to the original key speaks to the character's attempt to break free from the preconceived notions of her work. However, the fact the she ends in the key in which she began hints that, even after defending herself, she is still not certain that what she does is of enough importance. After all, she finishes the song with the phrase "just a housewife."

While Carnelia uses a limited harmonic palette as the foundation for the song, he uses rhythm to help propel the character forward. Notice in the first A section of the song (measures 1–24), the two-measure cell (measures 1–2) is articulated by a whole note in the first measure followed by two half notes in the second measure. This choice eases the character into the song with a slow, almost hesitant quality, as if the woman is not sure of herself or that she has much to say.

At the very end of the first A section (measures 21–24) Carnelia adjusts the rhythm slightly. Now the first measure features a half note followed by quarter-note articulations on beats 3 and 4. This slight change is used as the new motif for the second A section (measures 25–44). This variation gives the song a slight forward motion that begins to suggest that more thoughts and emotions emerge as the character begins to discuss her life.

At the end of the second A section (measures 41–44), Carnelia again introduces yet another slight rhythmic variation. He moves into full quarter-note articulations in both measures of the cell (measures 41–42). This drives the emotional energy of the piece with even more urgency. It is an apt choice that supports the character's rising anger at how others try to characterize her life.

Carnelia makes a slight change in the B section of the song (measures 63–94). While still giving strong emphasis to the quarter note, he reverts to the half-note articulation on beat 1 of the first measure (measure 63) and then returns to strong, full-chord, quarter-note articulations on beats 3 and 4 and all of the next measure (measure 64). In doing so, he continues the rhythmic build of the piece, but the strong half-note articulation at the beginning gives an almost declamatory feel to the lyrics as the character begins to defend and assert herself with lyrics such as "I don't mean to complain and all, but . . ."

Halfway through the B section (measure 79), Carnelia finally propels the rhythmic energy into eighth-note movement. Wisely, he accompanies this change with a half-step rise in key, which further expresses the power of the character's transformation, most clearly expressed in the lyric, "Did ya ever think, really stop and think, what a job it was, doing all the things that a housewife does?"

As Carnelia returns to the A section, he begins to *slow* his rhythmic build by returning to, first, quarter-note movements, then reintroducing half-note articulations, and finally, in measure 123, to whole-note articulations. In this way, he *eases* back out of the build, returning the character to where she started, "like my mother . . . just a housewife."

Melodically, Carnelia continues the conventions he has used as the foundation for the character's expression: simplicity and repetition. In the A sections of the song, the melody operates, unlike the accompaniment, in four-measure units (measures 5–8). The melody begins in measure 5 with a diatonic ascent on beat 2 (beginning on the dominant and rising to the tonic). In measure 6, he repeats the rest on beat 1, follows on beat 2 with a rise on G-sharp to the dominant, and falls on beat 3 to the F-sharp (the third of the tonic chord), and on beat 4 to the tonic. The G-sharp-to-A has been prepared by the introduction of the g-sharp in the accompaniment cell. In measure 7, Carnelia repeats the same pitches as in measure 5 (albeit with different rhythms obviously determined to help support the text) and in measure 8 repeats the basic melodic structure of measure 6 with the one exception of denying the cadential landing on tonic on beat 4.

Examination of the melody in measures 9–12 shows that Carnelia follows the same essential pattern with a few pitch adjustments to correspond to the new, dominant harmony.

These simple choices make the song familiar and predictable. The tune adopts an incessant, singsong quality. One suspects this may be Carnelia's intention. The listener gets caught up in the character's routine. But in the B section, Carnelia makes yet another simple choice that gives the song an important release from the mundane. Wisely, it comes as the character is beginning her transformation.

At measure 63, Carnelia anchors the melody to the dominant scale degree and turns the melody into an almost one-note diatribe. The only break in the intensity is the occasional dip down into the chromatic lower neighbor (that wonderfully useful G-sharp again!). The dip to the lower neighbor helps to propel and serve as a springboard for the character, almost as if she is gaining more and more courage and self-worth with each passing phrase. The power of this simple choice is evidenced on two fronts. Given that the melodic contour of the A section has been so carefully restrained, this change speaks volumes about the change occurring within the character. Further, Carnelia gets great mileage from this simple choice, continuing to use it even when he changes key within the B section itself.

And, at the return of the A section, just as Carnelia reverted to previously established rhythmic and harmonic patterns, so he now does melodically. In measures 103–124, he uses his original A-section melodic motifs, but rather than restate them literally he allows himself to use them in fragments. It is clear that the character is returning, but the slight variations keep the piece interesting and reveal that the character is a bit unsettled by her journey.

Carnelia demonstrates, with amazing potency, one of the most important principles for good songwriting for the stage: simplicity. If the goal is to express the character, Carnelia's careful restraint and reliance upon basic harmonic, melodic, and rhythmic ideas communicate the tedium, frustration, and reawakening of a humble housewife.

Just a Housewife

Music and lyrics by Craig Carnelia

Bb/D (addA) (addG) Bb/D (addA) (addG)

What I do is out of fash-ion. What I feel is out of date.

Ebsus2(no3) (addA) (addG) Ebsus2(no3) (addA) (addG)

All I am is some-one's moth-er. Right a-way I'm "not too bright."

Bb/D (addA) (addG) Bb/D (addA) (addG)

What I do is "un-ful-fill-ing." So the T. V. talk shows tell me ev-'ry

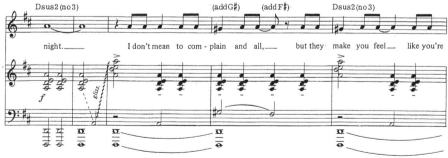

Dsus2(no3) (addG#) (addF#) Dsus2(no3)

night.____ I don't mean to com-plain and all,____ but they make you feel____ like you're

two feet tall__ when you're just a wife.__ Now - a - days all the mag - a - zines__ make a

bunch o' beans__ out o' fam - 'ly life.__ You're a whiz if you go to work,__ but you're

just a jerk__ if you say you won't.__ Wom-en's Lib says they think it's fine__ if the
*(Peo - ple say that they think it's fine)

choice is mine,__ but you *know* they don't!__ What I do; what I

*Alternate Lyric

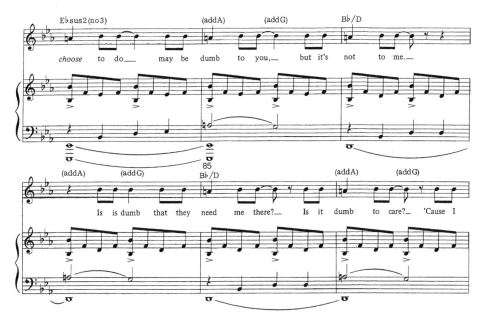

choose to do___ may be dumb to you,___ but it's not to me.___

Is is dumb that they need me there?___ Is it dumb to care? 'Cause I

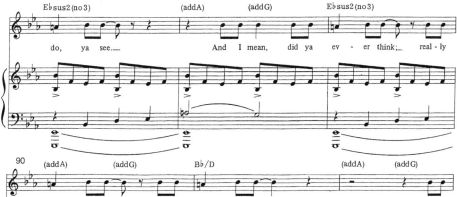

do, ya see.___ And I mean, did ya ev - er think;___ real - ly

stop and think___ what a job it was,___ do - ing

Major and Minor Mode as
Expression of Character and Subtext

It is generally agreed that, at a basic perceptual level, those who listen to Western music characterize the major mode as "happy, bright, or effusive," and the minor mode as "sad, dark, and introspective." Composers of program music (music intended to evoke extramusical images or ideas, generally instrumental works and without lyrics) employ a conscious choice. Musical theatre music and, in fact, music of all genres in which there is a character (protagonist) singing lyrics that are supported by accompaniment, offers deeper levels of interpretation. In this case, it can be compelling to consider the lyrics as putting forth the "real" text (that which is explicit), the melody stating a form of "subtext" (meaning behind the words), and the accompaniment providing yet another, more intense level of subtext.

An examination of "Love, Look Away" from the 1958 Rodgers and Hammerstein musical *Flower Drum Song* provides the listener with an example of a song from the vast musical theatre canon in which such possibility exists. One might consider the implied "minor mode" melody as representing the protagonist's bereft feelings of love unrequited, while the "major mode" inherent in the accompaniment speaks of the sublime beauty of love. The juxtaposition, major and minor, can be perceived as that "bittersweet" feeling that can accompany an intense emotion like love.

In the story, the character Helen is in love with Wang Ta, a man whose marriage with another woman is arranged. Helen sings the following lyrics as she realizes the hopelessness and folly of her situation:

> I have wished before,
> I will wish no more.
> Love, look away!
> Love, look away from me.
> Fly, when you pass my door,
> Fly and get lost at sea.
>
> Call it a day.
> Love, let us say we're through.
> No good are you for me,
> No good am I for you.
>
> Wanting you so,
> I try too much.

After you go,

> After you go,
> I cry too much.
>
> Love, look away.
> Lonely though I may be,
> Leave me and set me free,
> Look away, look away, look away . . . from . . . me.[2]

The song begins in the key of E-flat major. Helen's melody in the four-measure verse is on B-flat, the dominant. Preceding Helen's first utterance is a chord on the downbeat in the accompaniment that spells a I$_4^6$. The instability of both a dominant monotone melody and a second-inversion tonic triad leave the listener "dangling," awaiting resolution, in the same way that Helen seeks solace in her hopeless situation. The accompaniment progresses to a strong V^7 in the last two measures of the introduction and leads directly into the tonic on the downbeat of measure 5.

Helen's melody in measures 5–8 is a set of two minor triads, G-minor and F-minor. It is followed by a diminished triad in measure 9 and a minor-minor seventh chord in measure 11. When heard without accompaniment, a minor or "sad" sound is firmly established. It is interesting, however, that the accompaniment seems to tell another "tale." The downbeat of the chorus (measure 5) is a MM-9th sonority that belies Helen's feeling of desperation and focuses instead on the "richness" and "expansiveness" of an emotion like love. In fact, short of a one-measure foray into c-minor (the relative key of E-flat major), each section of the A section yields a clearly established home in E-flat major. Other compositional devices underscore the major mode of the accompaniment. In measures 7–9, and again in measures 15–16, an inner-voice tonic-upper neighbor-tonic countermelody reinforces the major key.

The lyric "me" in measures 8 and 18 falls first on the dominant pitch and then on the mediant. Taken by themselves, the two utterances appear to spell the root and third of a g-minor triad, underscoring Helen's despair. Yet, when she sings the word "you" in measure 20, she does so on a high tonic E-flat. It is the first time in the song thus far that an E-flat in the melody occurs with a tonic (and major) sonority. Once can interpret this as reflecting Helen's acute feelings for the object of her affection even as she acknowledges that the love will never be returned. Additionally, the lower-neighbor figure in the accompaniment (tonic-leading tone-tonic) reinforces the drama of her emotion, seeking, yet seeming to fall away from resolution.

The melody in the bridge presents an interesting contrast to that of the A sections. Whereas triads and seventh chords (all stacked in thirds) comprise nearly the entire A section, the bridge features diatonic movement, predominantly in an ascending pattern. In this part, the melody seems more "earthbound," almost plodding along, and creates a striking parallel to Helen's lyrics. Notice that, in the A sections, Helen places the burden of action on something outside of herself. In this case, love (the dramatic metaphor for Wang Ta). She asks love to "look away" and "fly," and the ascending leaps of thirds color those actions. When, in the bridge, Helen's action words become more self-directed—"wanting you," "I try," "I cry"—the text is painted with the aforementioned diatonic melody, and seem to reflect Helen's own feelings of being "earthbound," as she tries to go through her day in sorrow. Rhythmic patterns in measures 21–22 and 25–26 further strengthen the lamination of melody and lyric, as the accents become "displaced" and the pulse more "ponderous," almost behind the beat. They seem to parallel Helen's fatigue and hopelessness in the face of unrequited love. Even the bass line of the accompaniment in those measures descends in stepwise motion.

Upon the final statement of the A section, and at the climax in measures 33–36, the harmony (which thus far has stayed very close to I in E-flat major) finally leaves the major tonic, via mm-9th chord ($V^{(\flat)9}$/vi), and arrives at c-minor momentarily. This minor mode "agreement" between Helen's melody and the accompaniment occurs as Helen states what may be her difficult wish to "set me free."

The range of Helen's melody extends to a high G in measure 35 and features in the accompaniment, once again, a tonic sonority in second inversion, reflecting, in the final measures of the song, the lack of emotional resolution sensed in the introduction.

Helen's final vocalization is sung on a descending E-flat major scale. This ultimate downward melodic motion, in contrast to what has been primarily one of ascent, paints a dramatic musical picture of Helen's anguish.

For the majority of Rodgers and Hammerstein collaborations, Oscar Hammerstein would create the lyric to a song first, and then Rodgers would compose the music. Rodgers felt that "If a composer is to reach his audience emotionally—and surely that's what theatre music is all about—he must reach the people through sounds they can relate to."[3] The extent to which Rodgers charted the musical journey of "Love, Look Away" may not be known, but certainly the profoundly descriptive lamination of text and music speaks to Rodgers' and Hammerstein's genius at finding the most appropriate means to reach their audience emotionally.

Love, Look Away

Lyrics by Oscar Hammerstein II   **Music by Richard Rodgers**

I have wished be - fore. I will wish no more.

Love, look a - way! Love look a-way from me. Fly when you pass my

door, Fly and get lost at sea. Call it a day. Love, let us say we're through. No good are you for me, No good am I for

you. Want-ing you___ so, I try too much.___

Af - ter you___ go I cry too much.___ Love, look a - way,___

___ Lone - ly though I may be, Leave me and set me free,___ Look a -

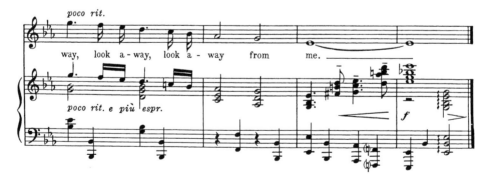

way, look a - way, look a - way from me.___

Musical Realization of a Misspent Life

An exploration of Jason Robert Brown's "Stars and the Moon" from *Songs for a New World* yields numerous possibilities for a deeper understanding of the *musico/textual* gesture and a more fully realized performance.

Judging from the key signature at the outset, the song appears to be in the key of G-Major or e-minor. It becomes apparent quickly, though, that the song is, in fact, in the mixolydian mode on D (D–E–F$\sharp$–G–A–B–C–D). The frequent use of a C-major sonority leaves the impression of subtonic harmony, but D-major as the home key is implied at cadences in measures 51–53, 99–101, and through the extended coda beginning in measure 168, with the alteration of c-natural to c-sharp (the leading tone of D-major). The text of the song is cast as a narrative—a story, if you will—that is best told in a voice quality that approximates speech. It might be that by avoiding the strong melodic relationship of leading tone to tonic and strong movement to harmonic closure, the "honesty" of "speaking" the tale *and* the storyteller remain "believable" in a way that *singing* in D-major might not.

The range of the A section is only a major sixth (A to F-sharp) that moves predominantly by whole step, and the speechlike intonation contour mirrors that of the words. The lyric at this point is little more than exposition (who and what). The range of the melody is extended only slightly in measure 25 with an octave leap, A to A. It corresponds with the lyric "and I was sure," and seems to bring attention to itself as being an important statement.

The verse has rhythmic patterns that follow natural speech as well. They are not "regular" in the sense that syncopations, ties, and some triplet figures are used almost randomly; therefore, important descriptive words are "landed" through rhythmic placement. In measure 14, for example, rather than casting the rhythm of "but his" as either quarter notes or eighth notes, Brown chose a triplet figure that spans two beats, leaving the impression that the phrase "but his smile" is almost an afterthought that trails off wistfully. Similarly, if one contrasts the rhythm in measures 9–11 with the parallel phrase in measures 17–18, it appears that the protagonist knows exactly what she[4] wants to tell us first (measure 10—"I met a man without a dollar to his name") about the object of the song (with a relatively straightforward quarter rest-eighth-dotted-quarter-eighth-rest-eighth rhythm). In measure 18, the rhythm of quarter rest quarter-tied-to-triplets leaves the impression that the protagonist is "thinking" about what negative quality (obviously out of a list of many) to mention next ("I met a man who had no yearn or claim to fame").

The chorus introduces a more active rhythmic display. As the protagonist quotes "him," the words come forth more aggressively and with a more regularly recurring pulse, almost as if "his" words are a well-memorized, oft-repeated sales pitch. When the singer reacts in measures 50–52 with the decision "you know, I'd rather have a yacht," there is a return to the initial melodic motif of the verse, more contained, more calm than the chorus.

Stars and the Moon is strophic, and each verse is merely a continuation of the singer's story—a litany, if you will—of a life possibly misspent. The listener feels the "honesty" of the story channeled through a melody and accompaniment that does not play on heightened musical/dramatic impulse to supplement the text.

An A-Mm 9th appears in the accompaniment in measure 149 and is repeated eight times in the coda. This extended "dominant" (A–C-sharp–E–G–B-flat) complements the text with which it associates, creating a sort of musical "conjunction" that parallels the storyteller's use of the word "and." It leaves open the possibility for heightened drama, but finally resolves to a cadence along with the singer's resignation that "I'll never have the moon." The accompaniment rideout mirrors the song's introduction, bringing full cycle the protagonist's life of being tempted by change, but never reaching for it, always returning to what is a given in his or her life.

Stars and the Moon

Music and Lyrics by Jason Robert Brown

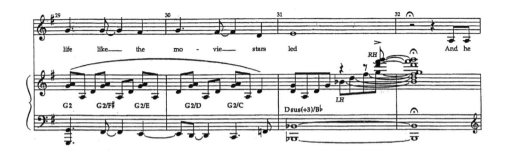

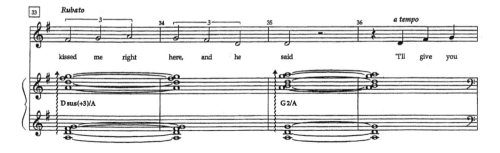

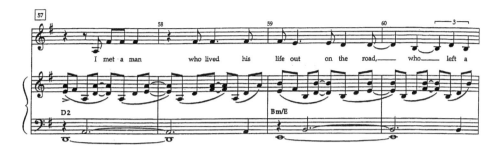

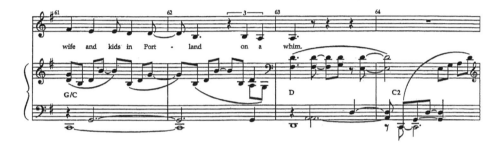

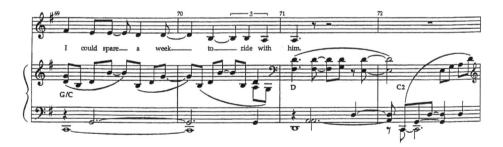

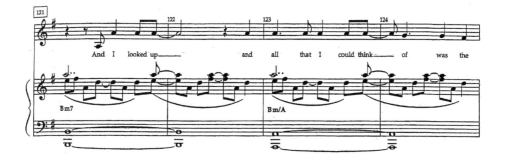

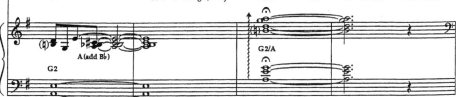

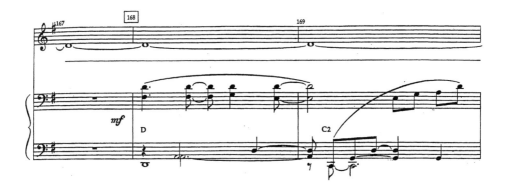

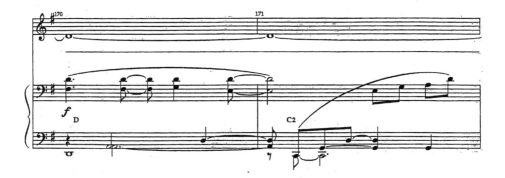

Having now examined several songs, questions arise. Are we, as interpreters, being presumptuous in assuming the authors' original intent? In offering models for study, are we mandating a specific interpretation of any song?

We maintain that the answer to both questions is a resounding "no." Certainly, one *does* risk dredging more meaning out of a song than may have been intended. At the end of the day, perhaps the significance of a particular compositional choice is just that it "sounds good." But, if one does not take the risk of reading too much into the music, one might not uncover myriad possibilities for interpretation and performance. In undertaking the task of finding meaning in musical theatre literature, designers, stage managers, directors, and performers are empowered to transport an audience to that realm where the *real* transcends the *unreal*.

Notes

1. Edward T. Cone, *The Composer's Voice* (Berkeley: University of California Press, 1974).

2. Oscar Hammerstein II and Richard Rodgers, "Love, Look Away," in *Flower Drum Song* (Milwaukee, WI: Hal Leonard, 1958).

3. Richard Rodgers, *Musical Stages* (New York: Random House, 1975), 273.

4. Jason Robert Brown has expressed his intention that the character singing this song "is meant unequivocally to be a woman." However, the authors believe that *any* text that does not explicitly state details such as gender, location, or historic period can be interpreted and executed out of context (as in a cabaret setting) and free the performer to create a personal "stamp" on a song or monologue, provided he or she has created a strong enough subtext to support decisions in aesthetics.

3

Workbook

The following workbook pages give the student an opportunity to practice writing and constructing musical concepts. The exercises reinforce the important principles of musical composition that were addressed in part 1. In order that the student can submit them to the instructor, *these* pages may be photocopied.

WORKBOOK—MAJOR SCALES

Given the starting notes below, construct the major scales. Do not provide key signatures, rather, include the appropriate accidentals next to the notes on the staff.

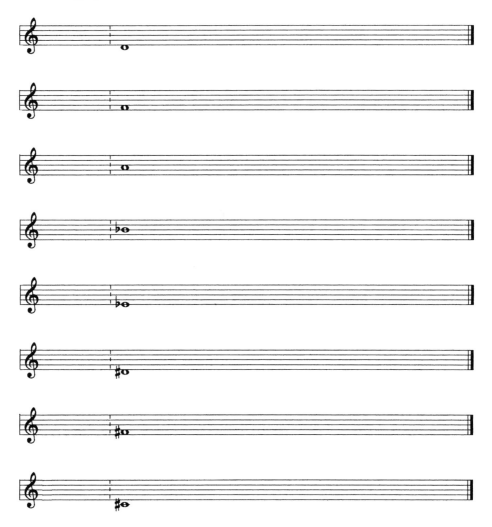

WORKBOOK—MINOR SCALES

Given the starting notes below, construct the minor scales as indicated. Be sure to include the ascending and descending version of the melodic minor scale. Do not provide key signatures, rather, include the appropriate accidentals next to the notes on the staff.

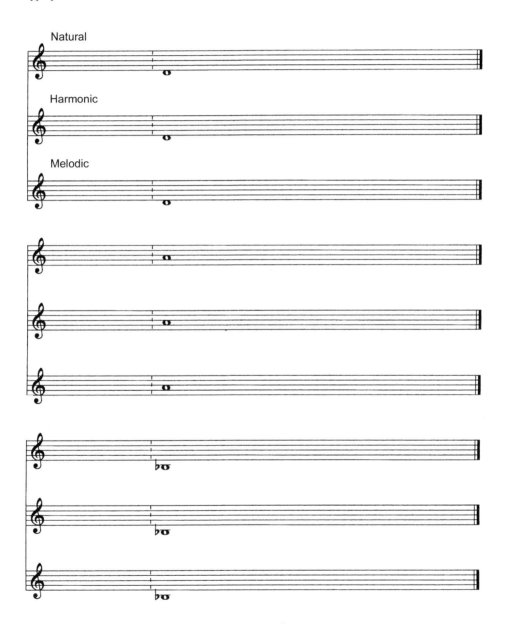

WORKBOOK—INTERVALS

Write the interval name under each pair of notes.

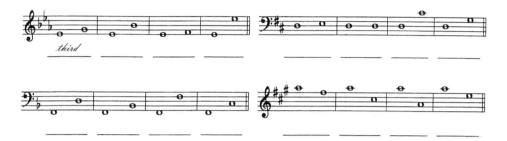

Draw the indicated interval above and below each printed note.

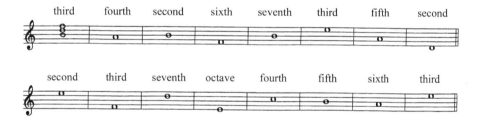

WORKBOOK—ENHARMONICS

Designate the enharmonic equivalents for the given notes.

WORKBOOK—KEY SIGNATURE

Reconstruct the Order of Sharps

Reconstruct the Order of Flats

Return to Workbook - Major Scales and Workbook - Minor Scales and now add the appropriate key signatures for the major and natural minor scales. (Do not add the key signatures for the harmonic or melodic minor scales.)

Provide the key signatures for the following keys:

A flat Major

C flat Major

d minor

C sharp Major

c sharp minor

B Major

Designate the correct major and minor keys for the following key signatures:

WORKBOOK—TRIADS

Build triads on the following major scales by simply adding the third and fifth above each root. Designate the mode of each triad on the line below.

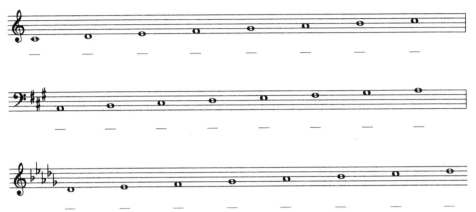

Build triads on the following minor scales by simply adding the third and fifth above each root. Designate the mode of each triad on the line below.

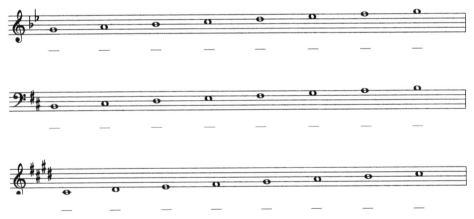

Draw a box around the major chords and circle the minor chords.

Add the appropriate accidental to the third of each traid to make it match the chord name.

E Major   D Major   A Major   c minor   f minor

Fill in the third and fifth above each root to build a major triad. Provide appropriate accidentials.

Fill in the third and fifth above each root to build a minor triad. Provide appropriate accidentals.

WORKBOOK—CADENCES

Identify each chord and then label the cadences.

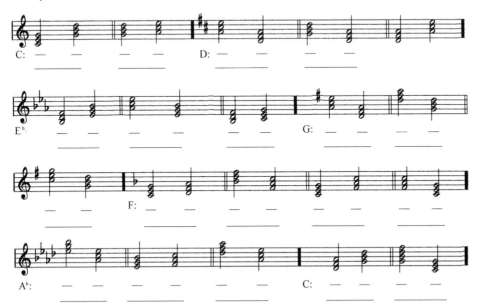

WORKBOOK—HARMONY

Write a Roman numeral under each chord in the following D Major progression.

D:

Now transpose the chord progression above to the key of B-flat Major. Identify each chord.
The first measure is complete. (Note clef change.)

B♭:

On the staves below, construct four harmonic progressions that capture different emotional sensibilities.

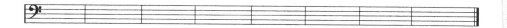

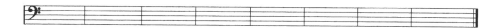

WORKBOOK—FUNCTIONAL AND
NONFUNCTIONAL HARMONY

On the staff system below, construct an harmonic progression and provide an entirely harmonic melody. Then replicate that harmonic progression on the second staff system and, still using the framework of your harmonic melody, add non-harmonic tones to expand the compositional interest.

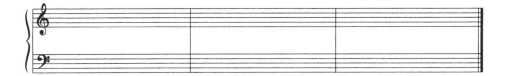

WORKBOOK—RHYTHM

In the measures below, create a rhythm etude which includes at least four different time sig
and all notes and rests up to the 32nd.

Glossary

abrupt modulation: Modulation moving suddenly from an established key to a new key, often a semitone or whole tone higher.

accidental: Character indicating chromatic alterations to pitches; commonly used accidentals include flats, sharps, naturals, double flats, and double sharps.

anticipation: Nonharmonic tone foreshadowing an approaching harmonic change.

appoggiatura: Nonharmonic tone sounding on a strong beat and then re-solving, chromatically or diatonically, immediately afterward.

augmented triad: Three-note chord containing two stacked major thirds, for example, C-E-G sharp. The interval between the root and the fifth is raised, "augmented," by one semitone.

authentic cadence: Cadence featuring a dominant (V) chord progressing to a tonic (I) chord.

bar lines: Vertical lines on the staff delineating measures.

bridge: The B section of an AABA song form (also called the *release*) that fea-tures contrasting music, often in a relative or parallel key, and provides reflection while preparing for the climactic return of the final A section.

cadence: Progression of two or more chords establishing the ultimate key of a musical section or phrase.

cambiata: A nonharmonic tone overshooting in the direction of resolution by a third and then resolving by step in the opposite direction.

chorus: The most memorable section of a musical theatre song. The text brings specificity to the notions expressed in the verse. A typical chorus is built of four eight-measure phrases. The most frequently found form is AABA, in which the A sections are exact or near-repeats of each other. The B, also called the *bridge* or *release*, features contrasting music, often in a relative or parallel key. The text of the bridge provides reflection and prepares the climactic return of the final A section.

chromatic scale: Scale built entirely of semitones.

coda: A short musical section serving as a finishing theme.

common chord modulation: Modulation featuring a chord that is common to, and can be analyzed in, both the established and destination keys.

common time: Time signature of $\frac{4}{4}$.

cut time: Time signature of $\frac{2}{2}$ wherein the half note carries the predominant beat and a faster tempo than $\frac{4}{4}$ is intended.

deceptive cadence: Cadence featuring a dominant (V) or dominant seventh (V⁷) chord progressing to a mediant (iii) or submediant (vi) chord rather than the tonic (I).

diatonic scale: Seven-note major or minor scale built on a combination of major and minor seconds.

diminished triad: Three-note chord containing two stacked minor thirds, for example, C-E-flat-G-flat. The interval between the root and the fifth is lowered, "diminished," by one semitone.

dominant: Fifth degree of any major or minor scale.

double flat: Character ♭♭ indicating the lowering of a pitch by two semitones.

double sharp: Character ✕ indicating the raising of a pitch by two semitones.

downbeat: First beat or primary accent of a measure.

duple meter: Rhythmic patterns featuring two beats to a measure or multiples thereof.

échappée: Nonharmonic tone that "escapes" resolution in the wrong direction by step and therefore resolves by a leap of a third in the right direction.

eleventh chord: Six-note tertian chord that features the root, third, fifth, seventh, ninth, and eleventh scale degrees.

enharmonic: Pitches sounding the same but written or notated differently, for example, d-sharp and e-flat.

enharmonic modulation: Modulation featuring a chord in the original key that can be respelled enharmonically in the destination key.

first inversion: Chord in which the notes are arranged with the third on the bottom and the root on the top.

flat: Character ♭ indicating lowering of a pitch by one semitone.

half cadence: Chord progression ending on a dominant (V) chord approached from a variety of possible chords.

harmonic minor: Natural minor scale featuring a raised seventh step and resulting in a leading tone.

harmonic tones: Tones drawn from the momentary harmony upon which they are sounded.

harmony: Simultaneous sounding of two or more pitches.

higher-order tertian (H.O.T.) chords: Chords built upon thirds featuring four or more tones, for example, sevenths, ninths, elevenths, and thirteenths.

interval: Distance (diatonic) between two notes.

introduction: Instrumental prelude; can be as simple as a single note providing a starting pitch for the singer or as complex as a multimeasure cell introducing a musical motif.

key: Sequence or organization of tones forming major or minor scales with particular attention paid to the relationship of all tones to the tonic.

key signature: Musical tonality indicated by the placement of accidentals at the intiation of a composition and any subsequent key change.

leading tone: Seventh degree of any major or minor scale that is one semitone below, thereby urging resolution to, the tonic.

major scale: Scale consisting of, from the tonic upward, two consecutive whole tones followed by one semitone, three whole tones, and one semitone (Starting Note/WT/WT/ST/WT/WT/WT/ST).

measure: Metrical divisions indicated by bar lines and the notes and rests contained therein.

mediant: Third degree of any major or minor scale.

melodic minor: Natural minor featuring raised sixth and seventh steps ascending and lowered sixth and seventh steps descending.

melody: Succession of individual pitches expressing musical contour and shape.

meter: Regular recurrence of alternating stressed and unstressed beats.

mode: Resulting color or tonality elicited from scales or melodic sequences, as in the distinction between major and minor modes.

modulation: Shift in key or tonal center characterized by a new dominant-tonic relationship.

mutation: Changing modality (major to minor or vice versa) without formally altering the key.

natural: The character ♮ canceling a previous alteration (sharp or flat).

natural minor scale: Scale consisting of, from the tonic upward, one whole tone followed by one semitone, two whole tones, one semitone, and two whole tones (Starting Note/WT/ST/WT/WT/ST/WT/WT).

neighbor tone: Nonharmonic tone serving as a melodic ornament that moves stepwise (diatonically or chromatically) away from and then back to a given harmonic tone.

ninth chord: Five-note tertian chord that features the root, third, fifth, seventh, and ninth scale degrees.

nonharmonic tone: Tone foreign to the momentary harmony upon which it is sounded.

octave: Interval spanning eleven semitones.

parallel keys: Key relationships wherein two keys share the same tonic pitch but have different key signatures, for example, C-major and c-minor.

passing tone: Nonharmonic tone occurring between two stepwise (diatonic) tones on an unaccented beat; passing tones may move in any direction.

pedal point: A tone that is sustained in the bass as harmony above changes.

perfect: Term applied to the intervals of a unison, octave, fourth, and fifth in a major or minor scale.

plagal cadence: Cadence featuring a subdominant (IV) chord progressing to a tonic (I).

relative keys: Key relationships wherein two keys share the same key signature but have different tonics a minor third apart, for example, E-flat major and c-minor.

release: See *bridge*.

rest: Duration of silence.

retardation: Nonharmonic tone forestalling, by melodic extension, a complete harmonic resolution.

rhythm: Pattern established by unit duration providing musical movement and animation.

rideout: An instrumental "tag" that punctuates the end of a song.

rondo: ABACA song form.

root: Synonym for the tonic or fundamental note of a chord.

scale: Stepwise sequence of semitones or whole tones; can be diatonic or chromatic.

secondary dominant: Subordinate chords built upon the fifth of a primary chord; for example, the secondary dominant of the tonic chord in C-major (C-E-G) would be the triad built upon the G (G-B-D).

second inversion: Chord in which the notes are arranged with the fifth on the bottom and the root and third on the top.

semitone: Distance between two adjacent pitches; a half step.

seventh chord: Four-note tertian chord that features the root, third, fifth, and seventh scale degrees.

sharp: Character ♯ indicating raising a pitch by one semitone.

strophic: Song forms that feature musical repetition.

subdominant: Fourth degree of any major or minor scale.

submediant: Sixth degree of any major or minor scale.

subtonic: Seventh degree of any scale which is one whole tone below the tonic.

supertonic: Second degree of any major or minor scale.

suspension: Nonharmonic tone sounding on a strong beat that is then tied or carried over into the resolution.

tempo: Relative speed of rhythm.

tertian: Concept of building chords in thirds.

thirteenth chords: Seven-note tertian chord that features the root, third, fifth, seventh, ninth, eleventh, and thirteenth scale degrees.

through-composed: Songs that are written with no sectional repetition.

time signature: Symbol indicating meter by specifying note values within measures.

tonic: First degree of any scale.

triad: Three-note chord containing the root and its third (major or minor) and fifth (perfect, diminished, or augmented).

triple meter: Rhythmic patterns featuring three beats.

upbeat: Final, unaccented beat of a measure just before a downbeat in a new measure.

verse: Typically following the introduction, the verse features expository text and its music serves as transition from speech into singing.

whole tone: Distance of two semitones.

Appendix

Permissions

Being Alive
from *Company*
Words and Music by Stephen Sondheim
Copyright © 1970 by Range Road Music Inc., Jerry Leiber Music, Mike Stoller Music and Rilting Music Inc.
Copyright Renewed
All Rights Administered by Range Road Music Inc.
International Copyright Secured   All Rights Reserved
Used by Permission

Can't Help Lovin' Dat Man
from *Show Boat*
Lyrics by Oscar Hammerstein II
Music by Jerome Kern
Copyright © 1927 Universal—Polygram International Publishing, Inc.
Copyright Renewed
All Rights Reserved   Used by Permission

Christmas Lullaby
from *Songs for a New World*
Music and Lyrics by Jason Robert Brown
Copyright © 1996—Semolina Farfalle Music
All Rights Reserved
Used by Permission

Chop Suey
from *Flower Drum Song*
Lyrics by Oscar Hammerstein II
Music by Richard Rodgers
Copyright © 1958 by Richard Rodgers and Oscar Hammerstein II
Copyright Renewed
Williamson Music owner of publication and allied rights throughout the world
International Copyright Secured   All Rights Reserved

Far From the Home I Love
from the Musical *Fiddler on the Roof*
Words by Sheldon Harnick
Music by Jerry Bock
Copyright © 1964 Jerry Bock Enterprises and Mayerling Productions, Ltd.
Copyright Renewed 1992
All Rights for Mayerling Productions, Ltd. Administered by R&H Music
International Copyright Secured   All Rights Reserved

I Don't Know How to Love Him
from *Jesus Christ Superstar*
Words by Tim Rice
Music by Andrew Lloyd Webber
Copyright © 1970, 1971 Universal/MCA Music LTD.
Copyrights Renewed
All Rights for the U.S. and Canada Controlled and Administered by Universal Music Corp.
All Rights Reserved   Used by Permission

I Enjoy Being a Girl
from *Flower Drum Song*
Lyrics by Oscar Hammerstein II
Music by Richard Rodgers
Copyright © 1958 by Richard Rodgers and Oscar Hammerstein II
Copyright Renewed
Williamson Music owner of publication and allied rights throughout the world
International Copyright Secured   All Rights Reserved

I'm Not Afraid
from *Songs for a New World*
Music and Lyrics by Jason Robert Brown
Copyright © 1996—Semolina Farfalle Music
All Rights Reserved
Used by Permission

Just a Housewife
Written by Craig Carnelia
Copyright © 1978 Big A Music LLC
Administered by A. Schroeder International LLC
200 West 51st Street, Suite 1009 New York, NY 10019
International Copyright Secured All Rights Reserved
Used by Permission

King Herod's Song
from *Jesus Christ Superstar*
Words by Tim Rice
Music by Andrew Lloyd Webber
Copyright © 1971 by Norrie Paramor Music Ltd.
Copyright Renewed
All Rights Administered by Chappell & Co.
International Copyright Secured   All Rights Reserved

The Little Things You Do Together
from *Company*
Music and Lyrics by Stephen Sondheim
Copyright © 1970 by Range Road Music Inc., Quartet Music Inc., and
Rilting Music, Inc.
Copyright Renewed
All Rights Administered by Herald Square Music, Inc.
International Copyright Secured   All Rights Reserved
Used by Permission

Love, Look Away
from *Flower Drum Song*
Lyrics by Oscar Hammerstein II
Music by Richard Rodgers
Copyright © 1958 by Richard Rodgers and Oscar Hammerstein II
Copyright Renewed
Williamson Music owner of publication and allied rights throughout the
world
International Copyright Secured   All Rights Reserved

Losing My Mind
from *Follies*
Music and Lyrics by Stephen Sondheim
Copyright © 1971 by Range Road Music Inc., Jerry Leiber Music, Mike
Stoller Music, Rilting Music, Inc., and Burthen Music Co., Inc.
Copyright Renewed
All Rights Administered by Herald Square Music, Inc.
International Copyright Secured   All Rights Reserved
Used by Permission

Matchmaker
from the Musical *Fiddler on the Roof*
Words by Sheldon Harnick
Music by Jerry Bock
Copyright © 1964 Jerry Bock Enterprises and Mayerling Productions,
Ltd.
Copyright Renewed 1992
All Rights for Mayerling Productions, Ltd. Administered by R&H Music
International Copyright Secured   All Rights Reserved

A New World
from *Songs for a New World*
Music and Lyrics by Jason Robert Brown
Copyright © 1996—Semolina Farfalle Music
All Rights Reserved
Used by Permission

Ol' Man River
from *Show Boat*
Lyrics by Oscar Hammerstein II
Music by Jerome Kern
Copyright © 1927 Universal—Polygram International Publishing, Inc.
Copyright Renewed
All Rights Reserved   Used by Permission

Side by Side by Side
from *Company*
Music and Lyrics by Stephen Sondheim
Copyright © 1970 by Range Road Music Inc., Jerry Leiber Music, Mike
Stoller Music, and Rilting Music Inc.
Copyright Renewed
All Rights Administered by Herald Square Music, Inc.

International Copyright Secured   All Rights Reserved   Used by Permission

Sorry-Grateful
from *Company*
Music and Lyrics by Stephen Sondheim
Copyright © 1970 by Range Road Music Inc., Jerry Lieber Music, Mike Stoller Music, and Rilting Music, Inc.
Copyright Renewed
All Rights Administered by Herald Square Music, Inc.
International Copyright Secured   All Rights Reserved
Used by Permission

Stars and the Moon
from *Songs for a New World*
Music and Lyrics by Jason Robert Brown
Copyright © 1996—Semolina Farfalle Music
All Rights Reserved
Used by Permission

You Are Love
from *Show Boat*
Lyrics by Oscar Hammerstein II
Music by Jerome Kern
Copyright © 1928 Universal—Polygram International Publishing, Inc.
Copyright Renewed
All Rights Reserved   Used by Permission

Index

accidentals, 2, 10, 88, 89, 101
"A New World," 35–36
augmented, 9, 10, 18, 19

bar line, 40, 101
beat, 42
"Being Alive," 23, 37–38
Bock, Jerry, 29
bridge, 38, 42, 101
Brown, Jason Robert, 29, 32, 35, 69, 86
cadence, 21, 35, 37, 96, 101; authentic, 21, 101; deceptive, 21, 102; half, 21, 102; plagal , 21, 104
"Can't Help Lovin' Dat Man," 27, 32–33
Carnelia, Craig, 52–55
"Chop Suey," 2, 19
chord, 17, 21, 95; progressions, 24–27, 97
chorus, 38, 42, 101
"Christmas Lullaby," 29, 30
circle of fifths, 12, 34
climax, 24, 37
coda, 42, 102
Cone, Edward, 45, 86
conflict, 35
consonance, *xi*
common time, 41, 102
Company, 22, 31, 37
cut time, 41, 102

Denouement, xi
diminished, 9, 10, 18, 19; fully, 22; half, 22
dissonance, *xi*
dominant, 8, 25, 34, 102
dominant seventh, 35, 37, 38
double flat, 2, 102
double sharp, 2, 102
downbeat, 102

eighth note, 40
eighth rest, 40
eleventh, 23, 102
enharmonic, 10, 35, 92, 102
exposition, 24

"Far from the Home I Love," 15, 16
Fiddler on the Roof, 15, 29
fifth, 9, 18, 19
flat, 2, 102
Flower Drum Song, 15, 19, 64, 86
form, 42
fourth, 9, 18, 19

Hammerstein, Oscar, 32, 46, 64, 66, 86
harmony, *xii, xiii*, 15, 17–40, 102; functional, 24, 98
harmonic progression, 24
Harnick, Sheldon, 29

"I Don't Know How to Love Him,"
    26–27
"I Enjoy Being a Girl," 15, 17, 31, 32
"I'm Not Afraid," 32
interval, 9, 91, 103
introduction, 42, 103
inversion, 20; first, 20–21, 102; second,
    20–21, 104

Jesus Christ Superstar, 13
"Just a Housewife," 52–63

Kern, Jerome, 30, 32, 28, 46–48
key, 10–14, 93, 103; parallel, 14, 15, 42,
    103; relative, 13, 42, 93, 104
Key Signature, 10–15, 93, 103
"King Herod's Song," 13, 14

leading tone, 8, 103
"Losing My Mind," 37
"Love, Look Away," 20, 34, 64–68, 86

"Matchmaker, Matchmaker," 29, 33
measure, 40, 103
mediant, 8, 103
melody, *xii, xiii*, 1, 15, 17, 103
meter, 40, 103; duple, 41, 102; triple, 41,
    105
mode, 4, 15, 18, 94, 103; major, 4, 5, 8,
    18, 64; minor, 4, 5, 8, 18, 64; natural
    minor, 5, 6; harmonic minor, 5, 6,
    102; melodic minor, 5,7;
    ascending, 7;   descending, 7;
    mixolydian, 69
modulation, 10, 34–39, 103; abrupt, 37,
    101; common chord, 35–36, 102;
    direct, 37; enharmonic, 36, 102;
    temporary, 38
Musical Stages, 86
mutation, 15, 103

natural, 2, 103
ninth, 23, 103
nonharmonic tones, 28–34, 103;
    anticipation, 29, 101; *appoggiatura*,
    32–33, 101; *cambiata*, 31, 101;

échappée, 30, 102; neighbor tone,
    31–32, 103; passing tone, 28, 104;
    retardation, 30, 104; suspension, 32,
    33–34, 104

octave, 8, 9, 103
"Ol' Man River," 38–39, 46–51
Order of Flats, 11, 93
Order of Sharps, 11, 93
ornament, 29

pedal point, 35, 52, 53, 104
perfect, 9, 18, 104
pitch, 1
protagonist, 64

quarter note, 40
quarter rest, 40

resolution, 24, 35
rest, 40, 104
rhythm, *xii, xiii*, 40–42, 99, 104
rideout, 42, 104
Rodgers, Richard, 20, 32, 64–66, 86
Roman numerals, 18, 97
rondo, 42, 104
root, 10, 19, 104

scales, 104; chromatic, 3, 102; diatonic,
    3, 4, 102; major, 4, 5, 8–11, 15, 18–19,
    88, 103; minor, 5, 89; natural minor,
    6, 8–10, 13, 15, 18–19, 89, 103;
    harmonic minor, 6, 19, 89; melodic
    ascending minor, 7, 8, 19, 89, 103;
    melodic descending minor, 7, 8, 19,
    89, 103
second, 9, 18, 19
semitone, 1, 2, 104
seventh, 9, 18, 35, 104
sharp, 2, 104
Show Boat, 3, 27, 30, 28, 46
Show Makers, The, xii
"Side By Side By Side," 22–23
sixth, 9, 18
Sondheim, Stephen, 5, 22, 23, 31, 37
Songs for a New World, 29, 32, 35

"Sorry-Grateful," 31
"Stars and the Moon," 69–85
strophic, 42, 42, 70, 104
subdominant, 8, 25, 104
submediant, 8, 25, 104
subtext, 64, 104
subtonic, 8, 25, 104
supertonic, 8, 104

tempo, 41, 104
tertian, 17, 21, 34, 103, 104
Thelan, Lawrence, *xii*
The Composer's Voice, 45, 86
"The Little Things," 5
third, 9, 18
thirteenth, 23, 104
thirty-second note, 40
thirty-second rest, 40

through-composed, 43, 105
time signature, 40, 105
Tin Pan Alley, 43
tonic, 8, 10, 11, 18, 24, 105
triad, 17, 18, 19, 94, 105
tritone, 10
upbeat, 41, 105

verse, 42, 105

Webber, Andrew Lloyd, 13, 26
whole note, 40
whole rest, 40
whole tone, 1, 2, 105
Working, 52

"You are Love," 3, 4, 30–31

About the Authors

John Bell is the chair of the Performing and Fine Arts Department at De-Sales University. He was formerly an associate professor of theatre and the musical theatre coordinator at the University of Central Florida. Professor Bell holds a master of fine arts degree in musical theatre from San Diego State University and a bachelor of music degree from Ohio Wesleyan University. Prior faculty appointments include director of music theatre and opera at James Madison University and associate professor of theatre at the University of Michigan–Flint.

Steven R. Chicurel is the chair and an associate professor of theatre at the University of Central Florida. He has a bachelor of music degree from Mars Hill College, master of music degree from the Peabody Conservatory of Music, the Johns Hopkins University, and doctor of musical arts degree from the University of Kentucky. Prior faculty appointments include associate professor and director of musical theatre at Northern Kentucky University and Mars Hill College. He is a certified course instructor with testing privileges and service distinction of Estill Voice International, and is also the coauthor of *Geography of the Voice: Anatomy of an Adam's Apple*.